LABORATORY MANUAL TO ACCOMPANY

Fundamentals of Information Systems Security

1E REVISED

JONES & BARTLETT
LEARNING

World Headquarters
Jones & Bartlett Learning
5 Wall Street
Burlington, MA 01803
978-443-5000
info@jblearning.com
www.jblearning.com

Jones & Bartlett Learning books and products are available through most bookstores and online booksellers. To contact Jones & Bartlett Learning directly, call 800-832-0034, fax 978-443-8000, or visit our website, www.jblearning.com.

Production Credits
Chief Executive Officer: Ty Field
President: James Homer
SVP, Editor-in-Chief: Michael Johnson
SVP, Chief Marketing Officer: Alison M. Pendergast
SVP, Curriculum Solutions: Christopher Will
Director of Sales, Curriculum Solutions: Randi Roger
Author: vLab Solutions, LLC, David Kim, President
Editorial Management: High Stakes Writing, LLC, Lawrence J. Goodrich, Editor and Publisher
Copy editor, High Stakes Writing: Katherine Dillin
Senior Editorial Assistant: Rainna Erikson

Reprints and Special Projects Manager: Susan Schultz
Associate Production Editor: Tina Chen
Rights & Photo Research Associate: Lian Bruno
Manufacturing and Inventory Control Supervisor: Amy Bacus
Senior Marketing Manager: Andrea DeFronzo
Cover Design: Anne Spencer
Composition: CAE Solutions Corp.
Cover Image: © ErickN/ShutterStock, Inc.
Printing and Binding: Edwards Brothers Malloy
Cover Printing: Edwards Brothers Malloy

ISBN: 978-1-4496-3835-1

6048
Printed in the United States of America
16 15 14 13 12   10 9 8 7 6 5 4 3

Contents

Ethics and Code of Conduct

The material presented in this course is designed to give you a real-life look at the use of various tools and systems that are at the heart of every network security analyst's daily responsibilities. Through use of this material, you will have access to software and techniques used every day by professionals. With this access come certain ethical responsibilities.

The hardware, software, tools, and applications presented and used in this lab manual and/or the VSCL are intended to be used for instructional and educational purposes only.

As a student in this course, you are not to use these tools, applications, or techniques on live production IT infrastructures inside or outside of your campus or organization. Under no circumstances are you permitted to use these tools, applications, or techniques on the production IT infrastructures and networks of other organizations.

You are required to conform to your school or organization's Code of Conduct and ethics policies during the use of this lab manual and any of the tools, applications, or techniques described within.

Preface

Welcome! This lab manual is your step-by-step guide to completing the laboratory exercises for the Fundamentals of Information Systems Security course.

Virtual Security Cloud Lab (VSCL)

For most of the exercises in this lab manual, you will use the Virtual Security Cloud Lab (VSCL) resource.

> **Note:**
> The Virtual Security Cloud Lab requires use of either **Windows Internet Explorer** or **Mozilla Firefox**. The Virtual Security Cloud Lab does not support Google Chrome, Safari, or Opera at this time.

The VSCL is a collection of virtual resources including Windows and Linux servers, Cisco routers, and applications like Wireshark, FileZilla, and Nessus that will allow you to perform all of the tasks in this lab manual as if you were performing them in a live production environment. The heart of the VSCL is a Windows Workstation desktop configured to give you access to the tools and resources you need for each lab, without any special setup on your part.

As noted in the following table, some of the exercises in this lab manual will be performed without using the VSCL. For detailed instructions on how to perform these exercises, please consult your syllabus or instructor.

How to Use This Lab Manual

This lab manual features step-by-step instructions for completing the following hands-on lab exercises:

VSCL	LAB TITLE
Yes	Lab #1: Perform Reconnaissance and Probing Using Zenmap GUI (Nmap)
Yes	Lab #2: Perform a Vulnerability Assessment Scan Using Nessus
Yes	Lab #3: Enable Windows Active Directory and User Access Controls
Yes	Lab #4: Configure Group Policy Objects and Microsoft® Baseline Security Analyzer (MBSA)
Yes	Lab #5: Perform Protocol Capture and Analysis Using Wireshark and NetWitness Investigator
No	Lab #6: Perform Business Continuity Implementation Planning
Yes	Lab #7: Relate Windows Encryption and Hashing to Confidentiality and Integrity
Yes	Lab #8: Perform a Website and Database Attack by Exploiting Identified Vulnerabilities
Yes	Lab #9: Perform a Virus Scan and Malware Identification Scan and Eliminate Threats
No	Lab #10: Craft an Information Systems Security Policy

Video Walkthroughs of Each Lab

Each VSCL-based exercise in this lab manual includes a video walkthrough that gives you a quick overview of every step and function. You can watch the video walkthrough prior to performing the lab exercise, and refer to it as necessary while you complete the lab. You can pause, rewind, and fast-forward the video walkthroughs if you need to take notes or spend extra time on a particular step or function. Consult your syllabus or instructor for information on where to locate the walkthrough videos.

Step-by-Step Instructions

You'll find it easy to complete these lab exercises by following the detailed step-by-step instructions. Each step is clearly broken down into sub-steps, and all actions you are required to take are noted in **bold** font. Screenshots are included to help you identify key menus, dialog boxes, and input locations. If you get stuck on a step, refer to the lab video, which follows the order of the steps.

Deliverables

At the completion of each lab, you'll be asked to provide a set of deliverables to your instructor. These deliverables may include documents, files, screenshots, and/or answers to assessment questions. The deliverables are designed to test your understanding of the information, and your successful completion of the steps and functions of the lab. For specific information on deliverables, refer to the **Deliverables** section at the end of each lab.

> **Note:**
> Some labs require the use of a word processor (such as Microsoft® Word) for preparing and submitting deliverables. If you do not have access to a word processor, you can use OpenOffice on the Workstation desktop of the VSCL to prepare your documents. It includes a word processor called Writer that has all the features necessary for creating documents for use in these labs.

File Transfer

At times, you may be asked to transfer to another computer files you have created while performing lab steps in the VSCL. This can be performed using the File Transfer function built in to the vWorkstation desktop of the VSCL. Instructions for preparing and sending files using the File Transfer function can be found at the beginning of the video walkthrough for the first lab in each course (in most cases, Lab #1).

> **Note:**
> Use of this lab manual or the VSCL **does not require use of the textbook**. If you have questions about whether a textbook is needed for your course, consult your instructor.

Perform Reconnaissance and Probing Using Zenmap GUI (Nmap)

Introduction

Hackers typically follow a five-step approach to seek out and destroy targeted hosts. The first step in performing an attack is to plan the attack by identifying the target and learning as much as possible about it. Hackers usually perform an initial reconnaissance and probing scan to identify IP hosts, open ports, and services enabled on servers and workstations. In this lab, you will explore the Virtual Security Cloud Lab (VSCL). You will learn how to access several different applications, including PuTTY and the Zenmap Graphical User Interface (GUI) for the Nmap Security Scanner application. You will use the data you uncover to plan an attack on 172.30.0.0/24 where the VM server farm resides.

Learning Objectives

Upon completing this lab, you will be able to:

- Access the virtual machines (server farm and workstations) needed for the labs in this course
- Use the vWorkstation to connect to the applications and virtual machines needed for this lab
- Plan an initial reconnaissance and probing attack on the Virtual Security Cloud Lab (VSCL)
- Use Zenmap GUI (Nmap) to perform an "Intense Scan" on the entire targeted VSCL infrastructure (172.30.0.0/24)
- Generate a Zenmap GUI (Nmap) port scanning report and submit it as part of the deliverables for this lab

TOOLS AND SOFTWARE	
NAME	**MORE INFORMATION**
FileZilla Server and FileZilla Client	http://filezilla-project.org/
Nessus	http://www.nessus.org/products/nessus
NetWitness Investigator	http://www.emc.com/security/rsa-netwitness.htm
PuTTY	http://www.chiark.greenend.org.uk/~sgtatham/putty/
Tftpd32	http://tftpd32.jounin.net/
Wireshark	http://www.wireshark.org/
Zenmap GUI	http://nmap.org/zenmap/

Deliverables

Upon completion of this lab, you are required to provide the following deliverables to your instructor:

1. Soft copy of the Zenmap GUI "Intense Scan" report in XML format;
2. Topology fisheye bubble chart in PDF format;
3. Lab Assessment Questions & Answers for Lab #1.

Hands-On Steps

1. This lab begins at the student landing vWorkstation virtual machine desktop of the VSCL, as shown here.

FIGURE 1.1

"Student Landing" VSCL workstation

> **Note:**
> The next steps help familiarize you with the applications available in the VSCL environment. You will open several different applications, explore the interface, and close the application.

2. **Double-click** the **Wireshark icon** on the desktop to start that application.

   Wireshark is a protocol analyzer tool (sometimes called a "packet sniffer"). It is used to capture IP traffic from a variety of sources. You will use this application in a lab later in this course.

FIGURE 1.2

The Wireshark window

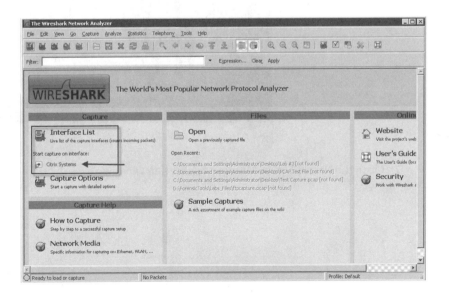

3. **Close** the **Wireshark application window**.

4. **Double-click** the **NetWitness Investigator icon** on the desktop to start that application.

   NetWitness Investigator allows you to look at and analyze packet capture data (collected by applications like Wireshark) in context, so that you are able to act on any threats or problems quickly and easily.

FIGURE 1.3

The NetWitness Investigator welcome screen

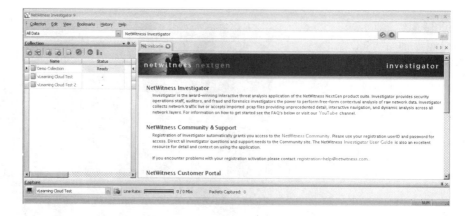

5. **Close** the **NetWitness Investigator application window**.
6. **Double-click** the **Nessus Server Manager icon** on the desktop to start that application.

   Nessus performs remote scans and audits of Unix, Windows, and network infrastructures and can perform a network discovery of devices, operating systems, applications, databases, and services running on those devices.

FIGURE 1.4

The Nessus window

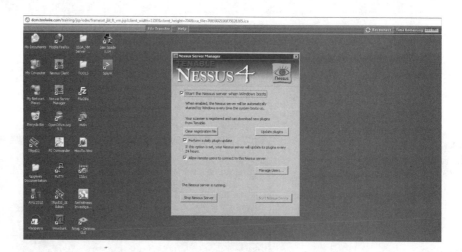

7. **Close** the **Nessus Server Manager application window**.

8. **Double-click** the **ISSA_VM Server Farm_RDP** icon on the desktop. This folder contains links to the virtual servers in this lab environment.

9. **Double-click** the **TargetWindows01.rdp file** to open the Windows Server.

FIGURE 1.5

Open a remote desktop
connection to the
TargetWindows01

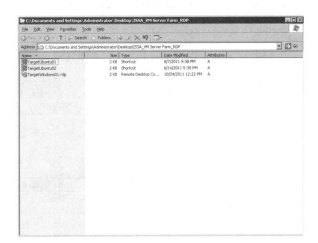

10. **Log on** to the **TargetWindows01 VM** server with the following credentials:
    - User name: **Administrator**
    - Password: **ISS316Security**

11. **Click OK** in the Connect to Server dialog box to start the FileZilla Server application.

    This dialog box loads automatically when the Windows server starts, with the address and password already filled in.

FIGURE 1.6

Connect to Server
dialog box

12. **Close** the **FileZilla Server application**.

13. Notice that many of the same application icons are found on the TargetWindows01 desktop.

14. **Close** the **TargetWindows01 window** to return to the vWorkstation desktop.

15. **Minimize** the **ISSA_VM Server Farm_RDP folder**.

16. **Double-click** the **FileZilla icon** on the desktop to start the FileZilla client application.

    FileZilla is an application that uses File Transfer Protocol (FTP) to send files to and from client and server computers.

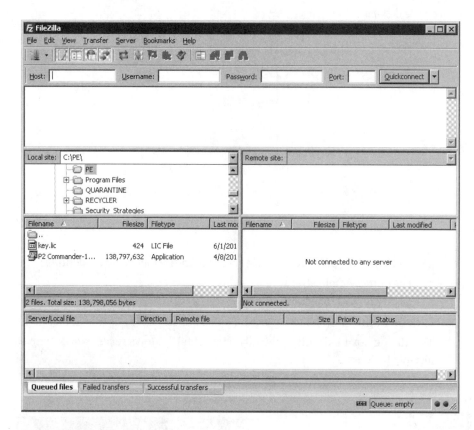

17. **Close** the **FileZilla Client window**.

18. **Double-click** the **Tftpd32_SE Admin icon** on the vWorkstation desktop to launch the application.

    The Tftpd32_SE application establishes one desktop as a TFTP (Trivial File Transfer Protocol) server and the other as a client so that files can be shared.

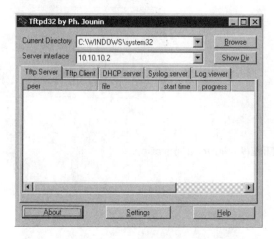

19. **Close** the **Tftpd32_SE Admin window**.

20. **Maximize** the **ISSA_VM Server Farm_RDP folder**.

21. **Double-click** the **TargetUbuntu01 icon** to open the lab's Linux Server.

22. Explore the menus to familiarize yourself with the environment.

23. **Close** the **TargetUbuntu01 window** to return to the vWorkstation desktop.

24. **Double-click** the **TargetUbuntu02 icon** to open the lab's Linux desktop.

25. Explore the menus to familiarize yourself with the environment.

26. **Close** the **TargetU buntu02 window** to return to the vWorkstation desktop.

> **Note:**
> The next steps will use the Windows Command Prompt using the ping command to verify that the target
> computer is accepting connections. You will also use PuTTY to make Telnet and Secure Shell (SSH) connections
> to the computers on the lab's virtual environment interface.

27. From the vWorkstation desktop, **click** the **Windows Start button**.

28. **Select Run** from the menu.

29. **Type cmd** in the dialog box and **click OK**.

30. In the Windows Command Prompt window, ping the IP address for the TargetWindows01 server.
    Type ping 172.30.0.8 and **press Enter**.
    The replies indicate that the Windows server is accepting connections.

FIGURE 1.9

Successful ping of
TargetWindows01

31. **Type ping 172.30.0.1** (the default gateway for this lab) and **press Enter**.
    The replies indicate that the gateway is accepting connections.

32. **Close** the **Windows Command Prompt window**.

33. **Double-click** the **PuTTY icon** on the desktop to start the PuTTY application.

34. In the PuTTY application window, **type** the IP address for LAN Switch 1, **172.16.8.5. Select** the **Telnet radio button** and **click** the **Open button** to start the connection.

PuTTY application
window

35. PuTTY will launch a terminal console window. At the login prompt, **type** the following:
- Username: **cisco**
- Password: **cisco**

PuTTY terminal console
window

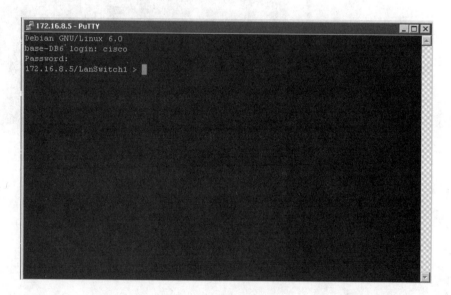

▶ **Note:**

The next steps involve using the Cisco IOS *show* command to obtain network documentation information from the interface you've connected to (LAN Switch 1). Cisco IOS is a package of routing, switching, and networking commands integrated with a Cisco-specific operating system, of which the *show* command is a key function. Entering a *show* command at the command prompt in the terminal console will return network information specific to the command you entered. There are hundreds of *show* commands in Cisco IOS; availability is based on the *privilege level* of the user. The relevant *show* commands for this lab include the following:

- *Show interface*: This command displays physical and logical configuration information about each interface and whether or not the interface is up or down. This commands tells you what interfaces are enabled and active;
- *Show IP interface*: This command displays logical IP address and subnet mask address information. It tells you what the IP subnet number, IP host address, and subnet mask address information is for all enabled ports;
- *Show IP ARP*: This command displays the address resolution table of MAC-layer addresses to assigned IP host addresses;
- *Show IP route*: This command displays the IP routing protocol used, the IP routes and network numbers visible to the switch/router, and the physical interface that an IP packet traverses based on the IP routes and IP networks seen (Cisco routers only);
- *Show VLAN*: This command displays the VLANs configured within the LAN Switch 1 and LAN Switch 2 devices only;
- *Show switch VLAN*: This command displays the VLANs configured within the ASA devices only.

36. In the terminal console window, at the command prompt labeled 172.16.8.5/LanSwitch1>, **type** the first Cisco IOS show command found in the Command column of the following table (**show interface**) and **press Enter**.

    Review the output for this command, being sure to look for the following information and use the data to complete the deliverables for this lab. Repeat this step for each of the show commands in this table.

COMMAND	DATA TO LOOK FOR AND REVIEW
show interface	Interface names, number of interfaces, interface up or down (available or unavailable)
show ip interface	Interface names, interface up or down, IP address, subnet mask address
show vlan	VLAN name, VLAN status
show ip arp	IP address, MAC-layer hardware address, interface name(s)

FIGURE 1.12

Data from Cisco IOS
show commands

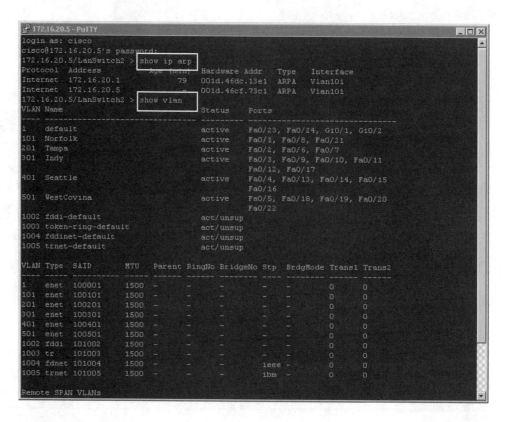

37. When finished entering the show commands and reviewing the output, **type quit** to close the terminal console.

38. **Double-click** the **PuTTY icon** to restart the application. This time, in the PuTTY application window, **type** the IP address for LAN Switch 2, **172.16.20.5**, select the **SSH radio button** and **click** the **Open button** to start the connection.

39. At the login prompt, **type** the following:
    - Username: **cisco**
    - Password: **cisco**

40. **Repeat** the show command entry process from Step 36, reviewing the returned output for the same data to complete the deliverables for this lab. When finished, **type quit** to close the terminal console.

41. **Repeat steps 38-40** using the IP addresses in the following table.

IP ADDRESS	COMMON NAME
172.20.8.1	West Covina
172.16.8.1	Norfolk
172.30.0.1	ASA_Instructor
172.30.0.8	TargetWindows01

Note:

The next steps use the Zenmap to perform a targeted IP subnetwork Intense Scan which will identify what hosts are available on the network, what services (application name and version) those hosts are offering, what operating systems (and OS versions) they are running, and what type of packet filters or firewalls are in use.

42. To start the Zenmap GUI application, **double-click** on the **Nmap-Zenmap GUI icon** on the desktop. The Zenmap GUI window opens with two drop-down menus labeled Target and Profile:

    • The Target field allows you to specify or select the networks or subnets you want to connect to;

    • The Profile field indicates the types of scans you can perform.

43. From the **Target drop-down menu**, **select 173.30.0.0/24**, the subnet address for this lab. From the **Profile drop-down menu, select Ping scan**.

44. **Click** the **Scan button**.

FIGURE 1.13

The Zenmap window

Review the output for this command, which returns basic information about host availability and the MAC address. You will need this data to complete the deliverables for this lab.

45. To gather more detailed data, **select 173.30.0.0/24** from the **Target drop-down menu**. **Select Intense Scan** from the **Profile drop-down menu** and **click** the **Scan button**.

> **Note:**
> The **Intense scan** can take 3 to 5 minutes to complete all 36 test scripts. When the scan has finished, Zenmap will display the **Nmap done** command.

FIGURE 1.14

Intense Scan of 172.30.0.0/24 IP subnetwork

46. **Click Scan** on the main toolbar and **select Save Scan** to save the scan results. When the Save Scan dialog box opens, **name** the file **Lab #1 Nmap Scan** and **select Nmap XML files [*.xml]** from the drop-down menu. **Save** to the file to the Security_Strategies folder (**My Computer > Local Disk (C:) > Security_Strategies**).

Saving the Lab #1 Nmap
Scan.xml file

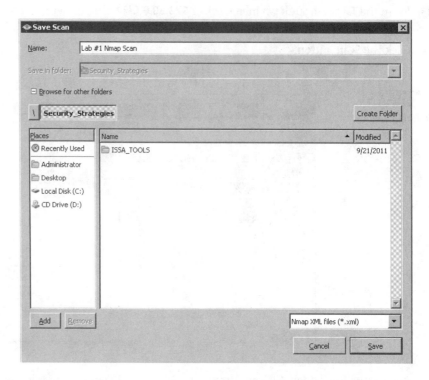

47. Review the output of the Intense Scan by **clicking** the **Ports/Hosts tab**. The data in this tab indicates whether ports are open and gives additional information about their state, service, and protocol. Continue to review the output, being sure to look for the following information in this table. You will use this data to complete the deliverables for this lab. Repeat this step for each of the tabs on this table.

TAB	DATA TO LOOK FOR AND REVIEW
Nmap Output	Raw Nmap outdata
Ports/Hosts	IP hosts and open ports
Topology	Fisheye bubble chart of IP hosts
Host Details	IP host OS fingerprint details
Scans	Completed scans performed

48. **Click** the **Topology tab**. This tab provides a fisheye bubble chart of all the IP hosts discovered during the scan. In this report, the bubble chart shows the relative size and connection type of all discovered hosts.

 Note:

A **bubble chart** is a type of graph used to show relationships, by size, of different variables across an X-Y axis. A **fisheye** lens is a tool which can be used to change the shape and orientation of the graph.

49. **Click** the **Controls tab** and use the **Zoom** and **Ring Gap** slider controls in the lower right corner of the window to adjust the size and orientation of the chart.

> ▶ **Note:**
>
> As you will be saving a copy of this chart for a lab deliverable, your goal should be to produce a graphic in which all of the hostnames and the relationship indicators are readable, without any overlapping hostnames.

FIGURE 1.16

Topology fisheye bubble chart

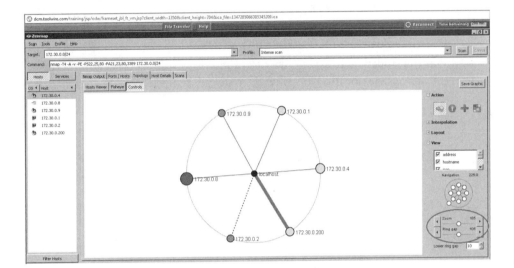

50. **Click** the **Save Graphic button.** You will need this file for the lab deliverables. When the Save Topology dialog box opens, **name** the file **Lab #1 Topology Fisheye Chart** and **select PDF** from the **Select File Type drop-down** menu. **Save** to the file to the Security_Strategies folder (**My Computer > Local Disk (C:) > Security_Strategies**).

FIGURE 1.17

Save graphic of your topology fisheye bubble chart

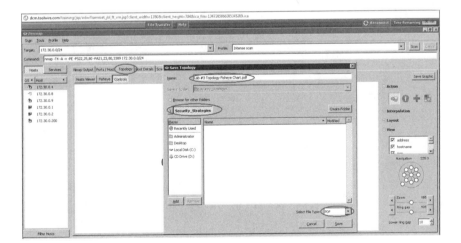

51. **Close** the **Nmap application** and **download** the **Lab #1 Nmap Scan.xml** and **Lab #1 Topology Fisheye Chart. pdf** files using the **File Transfer** button and **submit** both as lab deliverables.

Evaluation Criteria and Rubrics

The following are the evaluation criteria and rubrics for Lab #1 that students must perform:

1. Was the student able to access the virtual machines (server farm and workstations) needed for the labs? – [**20%**]

2. Was the student able to use the vWorkstation to connect to applications and virtual machines needed for this lab? – [**20%**]

3. Was the student able to plan an initial reconnaissance and probing attack on the Virtual Security Cloud Lab (VSCL)? – [**20%**]

4. Was the student able to use Zenmap GUI (Nmap) to perform an "Intense Scan" on the entire targeted VSCL infrastructure (172.30.0.0/24)? – [**20%**]

5. Was the student able to generate a Zenmap GUI (Nmap) port scanning report and submit it as part of the deliverables for this lab? – [**20%**]

LAB #1 – ASSESSMENT WORKSHEET

Perform Reconnaissance and Probing Using Zenmap GUI (Nmap)

Course Name and Number:
_____

Student Name:
_____

Instructor Name:
_____

Lab Due Date:
_____

Overview

Hackers typically follow a five-step approach to seek out and destroy targeted hosts. The first step in performing an attack is to plan the attack by identifying the target and learning as much as possible about the target. Hackers usually perform an initial reconnaissance and probing scan to identify IP hosts, open ports, and services enabled on servers and workstations. In this lab, students planned an attack on 172.30.0.0/24 where the VM server farm resides. Using Zenmap GUI, students then performed a "Ping Scan" or "Quick Scan" on the targeted IP subnetwork.

Lab Assessment Questions & Answers

1. Name at least five applications and tools pre-loaded on the TargetWindows01 server desktop, and identify whether that application starts as a service on the system or must be run manually.

WINDOWS APPLICATION LOADED	STARTS AS SERVICE Y/N
1.	❏ Yes ❏ No
2.	❏ Yes ❏ No
3.	❏ Yes ❏ No
4.	❏ Yes ❏ No
5.	❏ Yes ❏ No

2. What was the allocated source IP host address for the TargetWindows01 server, TargetUbuntu01 server, and the IP default gateway router?

_____

_____

_____

_____

3. Did the targeted IP hosts respond to the ICMP echo-request packet with an ICMP echo-reply packet when you initiated the "ping" command at your DOS prompt? If yes, how many ICMP echo-request packets were sent back to the IP source?

_____

_____

_____

_____

4. If you ping the TargetWindows01 server and the UbuntuTarget01 server, which fields in the ICMP echo-request/echo-replies vary?

_____

_____

_____

_____

5. What is the command line syntax for running an "Intense Scan" with Zenmap on a target subnet of 172.30.0.0/24?

_____

_____

_____

_____

6. Name at least five different scans that may be performed from the Zenmap GUI. Document under what circumstances you would choose to run those particular scans.

_____

_____

_____

_____

_____

_____

_____

_____

_____

_____

7. How many different tests (i.e., scripts) did your "Intense Scan" definition perform? List them all after reviewing the scan report.

_____

_____

_____

_____

8. Describe what each of these tests or scripts performs within the Zenmap GUI (Nmap) scan report.

_____

_____

_____

_____

_____

9. How many total IP hosts (not counting Cisco device interfaces) did Zenmap GUI (Nmap) find on the network?

_____

_____

_____

_____

10. Based on your Nmap scan results and initial reconnaissance and probing, what next steps would you perform on the VSCL target machines?

_____

_____

_____

_____

Perform a Vulnerability Assessment Scan Using Nessus

Introduction

In this lab, you will learn how to perform vulnerability assessments using Nessus, which is an application built specifically for network discovery of devices and the operating systems and software running on them. Nessus performs remote scans and audits of Unix, Windows, and network infrastructures and can perform a network discovery of devices, operating systems, applications, databases, and services running on those devices.

Learning Objectives

Upon completing this lab, you will be able to:

- Identify risks, threats, and vulnerabilities in an IP network infrastructure using Zenmap GUI (Nmap) to perform an IP host, port, and services scan
- Perform a vulnerability assessment scan on a targeted IP subnetwork using Nessus
- Compare the results of the Zenmap GUI "Intense Scan" with a Nessus vulnerability assessment scan
- Assess the findings of the vulnerability assessment scan and identify critical vulnerabilities
- Make recommendations for mitigating the identified risks, threats, and vulnerabilities as described on the CVE database listing

TOOLS AND SOFTWARE USED	
NAME	**MORE INFORMATION**
Nessus	http://www.Nessus.org/products/Nessus
Zenmap GUI	http://nmap.org/zenmap/

Deliverables

Upon completion of this lab, you are required to provide the following deliverables to your instructor:

1. Zenmap GUI scan report in soft copy with your notes on what you found;
2. Nessus vulnerability scan report in HTML soft copy;
3. Lab Assessment Questions & Answers for Lab #2.

Hands-On Steps

1. This lab begins at the student landing vWorkstation virtual machine desktop of the VSCL, as shown here.

FIGURE 2.1

"Student Landing" VSCL workstation

2. **Double-click** the **Nmap-Zenmap GUI icon** on the desktop.
3. From the **Target drop-down menu, select 173.30.0.0/24**, the subnet address for this lab. **Select Intense Scan** from the **Profile drop-down menu** and **click** the **Scan button**.

> **Note:**
> The **Intense scan** can take 3 to 5 minutes to complete all 36 test scripts. When the scan has finished, Zenmap will display the **Nmap done** command.

FIGURE 2.2

Intense Scan of 172.30.0.0/24 IP subnetwork

4. **Click Scan** on the main toolbar and **select Save Scan** to save the scan results. When the Save Scan dialog box opens, **name** the file **Lab #2 Zenmap Scan** and **select Nmap XML files [*.xml]** from the drop-down menu. **Save** to the file to the Security_Strategies folder (**My Computer > Local Disk (C:) > Security_Strategies**).

Saving the Lab #2
Zenmap Scan.xml file

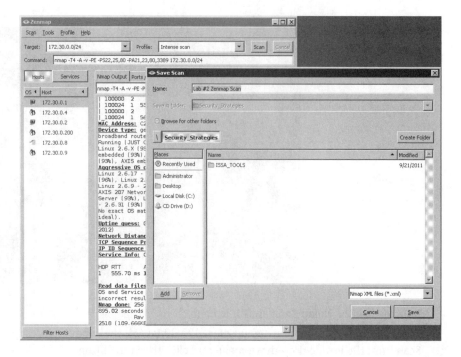

5. **Close** the **Nmap application** and **download the Lab #2 Zenmap Scan.xml** file using the **File Transfer** button and **submit** it as a lab deliverable.
6. **Double-click** the **Nessus Server Manager icon** to launch the application.

The VSCL "Landing"
vWorkstation:
Connecting to Nessus

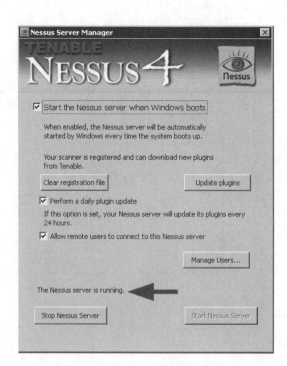

Verify that the Nessus server is running.

7. **Click** the **Manage Users button** on the Nessus Server Manager window to add a new user account.

8. In the Nesssus User Management dialog box, **click** on the **+ button** in the bottom left corner to open the **Add/Edit a user** dialog box.

9. **Type** the following logon information:
   - User name: **student**
   - Password: **ISS316Security**
   - Password (again): **ISS316Security**

10. **Select** the **Administrator checkbox** to give this user administrative privileges.

FIGURE 2.5

Add/Edit a user in
Nessus Server Manager

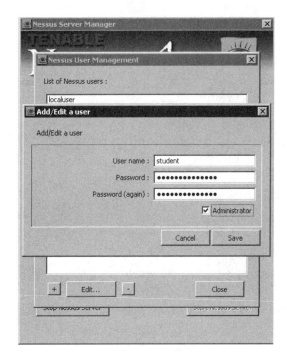

11. **Click** the **Save** button to finish creating the new user account, and then click **Close**.

12. **Close** the **Nessus Server Manager window**.

13. **Double-click** the **Mozilla Firefox icon** on the vWorkstation desktop to start the browser.

14. The Nessus client is accessed using a secure Web browser connection. **Type** the following URL in the Firefox navigation bar to open the locally hosted Nessus implementation, and then **press Enter**:

   • **https://localhost:8834**

> **Note:**
> The first time you connect to the Nessus client, you will see a Web page that tells you that the connection you are about to make is untrusted. To proceed any further, you must add Nessus to Firefox's exception list.

FIGURE 2.6

Untrusted connection dialog for Nessus server

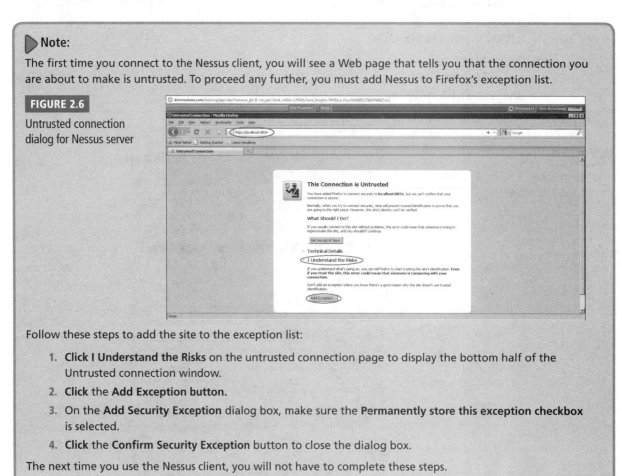

Follow these steps to add the site to the exception list:

1. **Click I Understand the Risks** on the untrusted connection page to display the bottom half of the Untrusted connection window.
2. **Click** the **Add Exception button.**
3. On the **Add Security Exception** dialog box, make sure the **Permanently store this exception checkbox** is selected.
4. **Click** the **Confirm Security Exception** button to close the dialog box.

The next time you use the Nessus client, you will not have to complete these steps.

15. When the Nessus client site appears, log in using the new user account you created in step 9:
   • User name: **student**
   • Password: **ISS316Security**

FIGURE 2.7

Log in to Nessus

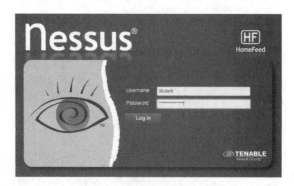

16. **Click** the **Log In button.**

17. **Click OK** to accept the Nessus HomeFeed Terms of Use and open the Nessus client homepage.

FIGURE 2.8

Nessus client homepage

> **Note:**
> The next steps will create a custom security policy using the Nessus client. This step, which configures the parameters for the scan, is required prior to conducting a vulnerability scan. The security policy includes:
>
> - Parameters that control technical aspects of the scan such as timeouts, number of hosts, type of port scanner, and more
> - Credentials for local scans (e.g., Windows, SSH), authenticated Oracle Database scans, HTTP, FTP, POP, IMAP, or Kerberos-based authentication
> - Granular family or plug-in-based scan specifications
> - Database compliance policy checks, report verbosity, service detection scan settings, Unix compliance checks, and more.

18. **Click** the **Policies tab** on the Nessus client homepage.
19. **Click** the **Add button** to add a new policy.
20. In the **Name** box, **type Lab #2 Policy**.

FIGURE 2.9

Creating Lab #2 Policy

Note:
Note that there are four configuration tabs: General, Credentials, Plugins, and Preferences. For most environments, the default settings do not need to be modified, but selecting one of these tabs will provide options for more granular control over the Nessus scanner operation as described in the table.

TAB	CONFIGURABLE OPTIONS
General	Allows you to name your policy and define the scan-related operations.
Credentials	Allows you to configure the Nessus scanner to use authentication credentials during scanning. By configuring credentials, it allows Nessus to perform a wider variety of checks that result in more accurate scan results.
Plugins	Enables the user to choose specific security checks by plug-in family or individual checks.
Preferences	Displays further configuration items for the selected category. This is a dynamic list of configuration options that is dependent on the plug-in feed, audit policies, and additional functionality that the connected Nessus scanner has access to.

21. **Click** the **Next button** to accept the default settings for the **General tab** and display the **Credentials tab**. Explore the configuration options, but do not make any adjustments or change any fields. **Repeat** this step for the remaining tabs described in the table.

22. Save the **Lab #2 Policy** parameters by clicking **Submit** on the final screen.

 Note:
The next steps will set up a vulnerability scan and create a scan report.

23. **Click** the **Scans tab** on the Nessus client homepage.

24. **Click** the **Add button** to add a new scan and configure the information described in the table.

FIELD LABEL	CONFIGURABLE OPTIONS
Name	Sets the name that will be displayed in the Nessus UI to identify the scan.
Type	Choose between Run Now (immediately execute the scan after submitting) or Template (save as a template for repeat scanning).
Policy	Select a previously created policy that the scan will use to set parameters controlling Nessus server scanning behavior.
Scan Targets	Targets can be entered by single IP address (192.168.0.1), IP range (192.168.0.1-192.168.0.255), subnet with CIDR notation (192.168.0.0/24), or resolvable host (www.Nessus.org).
Targets File	A text file with a list of hosts can be imported by clicking on Browse and selecting a file from the local machine. Example host file formats and individual hosts include: • 192.168.0.100, 192.168.0.101, 192.168.0.102 • Host range: 192.168.0.100-192.168.0.102 • Host CIDR block: 192.168.0.1/24

25. In the **Name** box, **type Lab #2 Server Farm Scan**.

26. In the **Type** box, **select Run Now** from the drop-down menu.

27. In the **Policy** box, **select Lab #2 Policy** from the drop-down menu.

28. In the **Scan Targets** box, **type 172.30.0.0/24** (the subnet address for this lab).

29. Leave the **Targets File** box empty.

FIGURE 2.10

Creating parameters for
Lab #2 Server Farm Scan

30. **Click** the **Launch Scan button** to start the scan.

   The scan will begin immediately and a yellow progress bar will indicate status.

FIGURE 2.11

Lab #2 Nessus Scan
progress bar

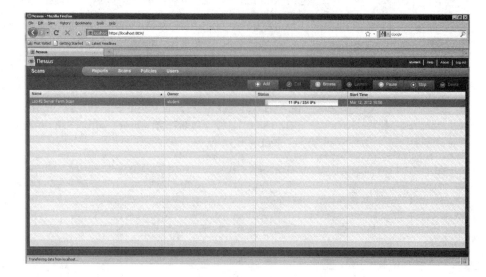

> **Note:**
> You can use the control buttons at the top of the Scans screen to Pause, Resume, or Stop the scan. Use the Browse button to see more detail about the progress of the scan for each target being scanned.

31. **Click** the **Reports tab** in the toolbar at the top to show the running and completed scans. The Reports screen acts as a central point for viewing, comparing, uploading, and downloading scan results.

32. **Double-click** the **Lab #2 Server Farm Scan** line item to open the report for that scan.

   The first screen you see is the summary screen, which gives an overview of hosts scanned and vulnerabilities discovered. Vulnerabilities are categorized according to severity: High, Medium, and Low.

> **Note:**
> You can also access the scan report by first clicking on the report name and then clicking the Browse button.

FIGURE 2.12

Nessus report summary

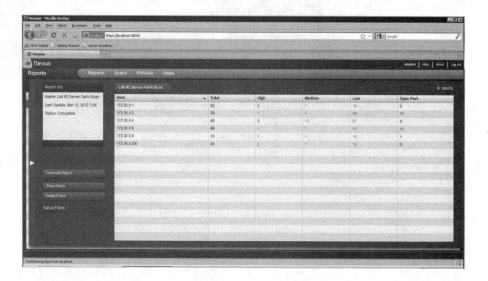

33. **Click** the **High column header** to sort the Hosts by vulnerability level. This will display the host with the greatest number of high-severity vulnerabilities at the top of the list.

> ▷ **Note:**
> Clicking a column header will toggle the displayed results either in descending order (greatest to least) or in ascending order (least to greatest). If you clicked the High column header in step 33 and found your results displayed in ascending order, click the column header again to change the order and proceed to the next step.

34. **Double-click** the host at the top of the list to open the report's detail screen.

    Just below the Nessus toolbar, on the Reports screen, you will see a "breadcrumb trail" of report pages. This trail is displayed as a series of clickable arrows.

FIGURE 2.13

"Breadcrumb trail" of Nessus reports

35. On the host detail screen, sort the port numbers by severity level by **clicking** the **High column header**.

36. **Click** TCP port number **443**, and then click on an individual error to see the full details of the finding, including a technical description, references, solution, detailed risk factor, and any relevant output. The details in the vulnerability Plugin ID provides overview, solution, risk factor, and CVE listing information.

FIGURE 2.14

Summary of findings for Port 443

37. **Click** the **Lab #2 Server Farm Scan arrow** in the breadcrumb trail at the top of the report to return to the report summary homepage.

38. **Click** the **Download Report button** on the left-hand menu to save a copy of the report. You will need this file for the deliverables of this lab.

39. In the Download Report dialog box, **select HTML export** from the drop-down menu and **click Submit**.

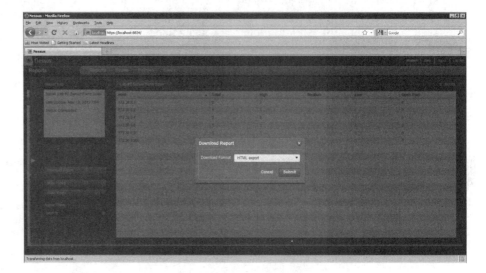

40. **Make a screen capture** of the front page of the **HTML report** and **paste** it into a text document. **Submit** it to your instructor as a deliverable. Make sure to show the listing of all IP hosts.

> **Note:**
> To capture the screen, **press** the **Ctrl** and **PrtSc** keys together, and then **use Ctrl + V** to paste the image into a Word or other word processor document.

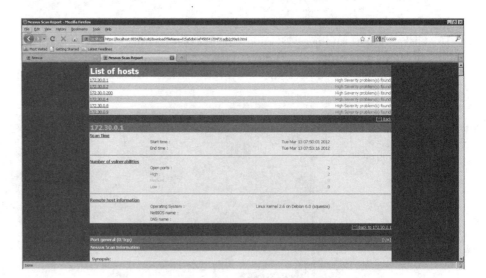

41. **Save** to the document to the Security_Strategies folder (**My Computer > Local Disk (C:) > Security_Strategies**).

42. Use the **File Transfer button** on the vWorkstation desktop to transfer the document to your physical workstation.

43. **Close** the **Firefox browser window** to exit the Nessus client.

44. **Close** the **Nessus Server Manager**.

Evaluation Criteria and Rubrics

The following are the evaluation criteria and rubrics for Lab #2 that the students must perform:

1. Was the student able to identify risks, threats, and vulnerabilities in an IP network infrastructure using Zenmap GUI (Nmap) to perform an IP host, port, and services scan? – [**20%**]

2. Was the student able to perform a vulnerability assessment scan on a targeted IP subnetwork using Nessus? – [**20%**]

3. Was the student able to compare the results of the Zenmap GUI "Intense Scan" with a Nessus vulnerability assessment scan and make a distinction? – [**20%**]

4. Was the student able to assess the findings of the vulnerability assessment scan and identify critical vulnerabilities? – [**20%**]

5. Was the student able to make recommendations for mitigating the identified risks, threats, and vulnerabilities as described by the CVE listing for the found vulnerabilities? – [**20%**]

LAB #2 – ASSESSMENT WORKSHEET

Perform a Vulnerability Assessment Scan Using Nessus

Course Name and Number:
_____

Student Name:
_____

Instructor Name:
_____

Lab Due Date:
_____

Overview

This lab demonstrated the first three steps in the hacking process that is typically performed when conducting ethical hacking or penetration testing. The first step in the hacking process is to perform an IP host discovery and port/services scan (Step 1: Reconnaissance and Probing) on a targeted IP subnetwork using Zenmap GUI (Nmap) security scanning software. The second step in the hacking process is to perform a vulnerability assessment scan (Step 2: Scanning) on the targeted IP subnetwork using Nessus vulnerability assessment scanning software. Finally, the third step in the hacking process (Step 3: Enumeration) is to identify information pertinent to the vulnerabilities found to exploit the vulnerability.

Lab Assessment Questions & Answers

1. What is the application Zenmap GUI typically used for? Describe a scenario in which you would use this type of application.

_____

_____

_____

_____

2. What is the relationship between risks, threats, and vulnerabilities as it pertains to information systems security throughout the seven domains of a typical IT infrastructure?

_____

_____

_____

_____

3. Which application is used for Step 2 in the hacking process to perform a vulnerability assessment scan?

_____

_____

_____

_____

4. Before you conduct an ethical hacking process or penetration test on a live production network, what must you do prior to performing the reconnaissance, probing, and scanning procedures?

_____

_____

_____

_____

5. What is a CVE listing? Who hosts and who sponsors the CVE database listing website?

_____

_____

_____

_____

6. Can Zenmap GUI detect which operating systems are present on IP servers and workstations? What would that option look like in the command line if running a scan on 172.30.0.10?

_____

_____

_____

_____

7. If you have scanned a live host and detected that it is running Windows XP workstation OS, how would you use this information for performing a Nessus vulnerability assessment scan?

_____

_____

_____

_____

8. Once a vulnerability is identified by Nessus, where can you check for more information regarding the identified vulnerability, exploits, and the risk mitigation solution?

_____

_____

_____

_____

9. What is the major difference between Zenmap GUI and Nessus?

_____

_____

_____

_____

10. Why do you need to run both Zenmap GUI and Nessus to perform the first three steps of the hacking process?

_____

_____

_____

_____

Enable Windows Active Directory and User Access Controls

LAB
3

Introduction

Windows Active Directory has five parts: domain services (manages users, groups, and more), rights management services (manages permission rights), federation services (manages identities across partner organizations), certificate services (manages certificates and encrypts data), and the lightweight directory services (manages directory services for other applications). In this lab, you will use the Windows Active Directory to create new users and groups with custom permission rights.

Learning Objectives

Upon completing this lab, you will be able to perform the following:

- Design a Windows Active Directory and user access control framework
- Create a new Windows Active Directory domain controller
- Evaluate existing user and group permission rights in Active Directory user accounts and their workstations
- Create new Windows Active Directory users and groups with custom permission rights
- Create and verify access control lists to protect objects and folders from unauthorized access

TOOLS AND SOFTWARE USED	
NAME	**MORE INFORMATION**
Windows Active Directory	http://www.microsoft.com/en-us/server-cloud/windows-server/active-directory.aspx

Deliverables

Upon completion of this lab, you are required to provide the following deliverables to your instructor:

1. Text document outlining the Active Directory tree created;
2. Text document with screenshot captures of successful and unsuccessful file writing;
3. Lab Assessment Questions & Answers for Lab #3.

Hands-On Steps

1. This lab begins at the student landing vWorkstation virtual machine desktop of the VSCL, as shown here.

FIGURE 3.1

"Student Landing" VSCL workstation

2. **Double-click** the **ISSA_VM Server Farm_RDP icon** on the desktop. This folder contains links to the virtual servers in this lab environment.
3. **Double-click** the **TargetWindows01.rdp file** to open the Windows Server.

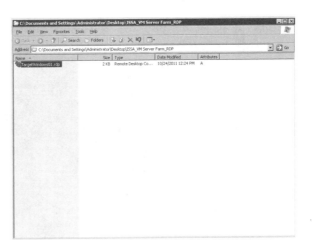

FIGURE 3.2

Open a remote desktop connection to the TargetWindows01

4. **Log on** to the **TargetWindows01 VM** server with the following credentials:
   - User name: **Administrator**
   - Password: **ISS316Security**
   - Log on to: **VLABS**
5. **Click OK** in the Connect to Server dialog box to start the FileZilla Server application.

   This dialog box loads automatically when the Windows server starts, with the address and password already filled in.

FIGURE 3.3

Connect to Server dialog box

6. **Close** the **FileZilla Server application**.

> **Note:**
> The next steps will use Active Directory to create a series of global domain groups.

7. **Double-click** the **Active Directory Users and Computer icon**.

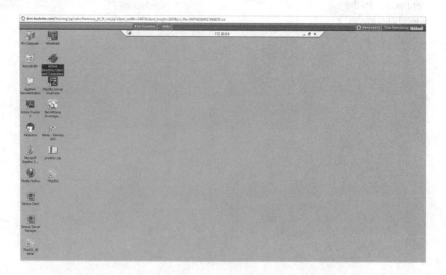

FIGURE 3.4

The TargetWindows01 desktop: Connecting to Active Directory

8. **Click** the **Users icon** in the left pane of the Active Directory window and then **click** the **Add a new group in the current container button** on the toolbar.

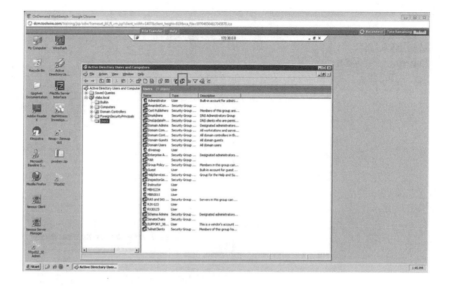

FIGURE 3.5

The Create new group icon in the Active Directory window

9. In the New Object - Group dialog box, **type Shopfloor** in the Group name box.

The Group name (pre-Windows 2000) box will populate with the new Shopfloor name as well.

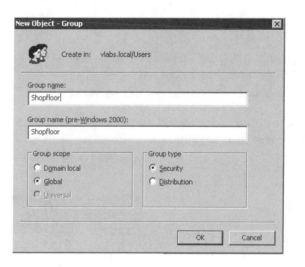

FIGURE 3.6

Add a new group in Active Directory

3

Enable Windows Active Directory
and User Access Controls

10. **Verify** that the Group scope is Global and the Group type is Security. Then, **click OK** to create the new global security group.

The new group, Shopfloor, has been added to the list of Users in the right pane.

FIGURE 3.7

New group added to
Active Directory

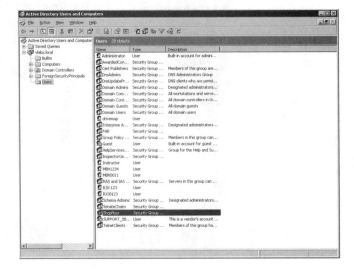

11. **Repeat steps 8-10** to create the following new global security groups:
    a. **Manager**
    b. **HumanResources**

> **Note:**
> The next steps will use Active Directory to create a series of new users and add them to the global security groups you created in the previous steps.

12. **Click** the **Users icon** in the left pane of the Active Directory window and then **click** the **Add a new user in the current container button** on the toolbar.

FIGURE 3.8

The New Object –
User dialog box

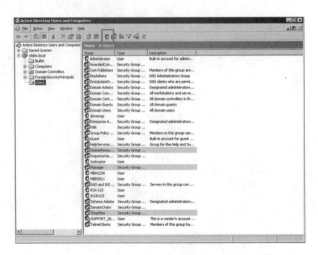

13. **Type** the following information in the New Object – User dialog box and **click Next** to continue:
   a. First name: **SFUser**
   b. Last name: **01**
   c. User logon name: **SFUser01**

   The Full name and User logon name (pre-Windows 2000) boxes will populate automatically.

FIGURE 3.9

The New Object –
User dialog box

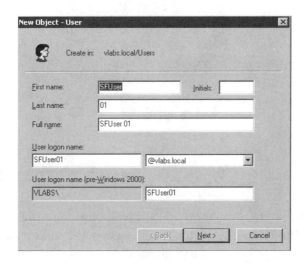

14. Type the following information in the password screen:
   - Password: **ISS316Security**
   - Confirm password: **ISS316Security**
15. **Click** the **User must change password at next logon checkbox** to remove the check. **Verify** that all of the checkboxes are unchecked.

FIGURE 3.10

Create a password
for a new user

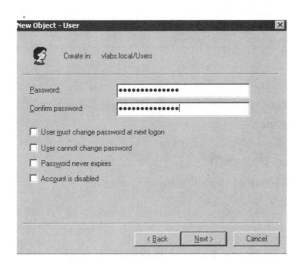

3

Enable Windows Active Directory
and User Access Controls

16. **Click Next** to continue.
17. **Click Finish** to create the new user account.

FIGURE 3.11

Click Finish to create the
new user account

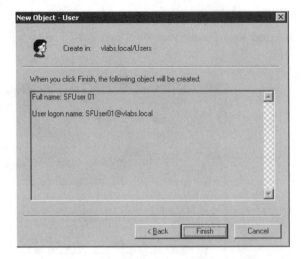

18. The new user name appears in the right pane with the groups you created earlier.
19. **Right-click** the **SFUser01** and **select Add to a group** from the context menu.
20. In the Select Group dialog box, **type Shopfloor** in the Enter the object name to select box.

FIGURE 3.12

Add a user to an
existing group

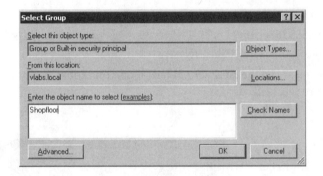

21. **Click OK** to complete the process.
22. **Repeat steps 12-18** to create the following new user:
    a. First name: **Manager**
    b. Last name: **01**
    c. User logon name: **Manager01**
23. **Repeat steps 12-18** to create the following new user:
    a. First name: **HRUser**
    b. Last name: **01**
    c. User logon name: **HRUser01**
24. **Repeat steps 19-21** to **add Manager01 to the Shopfloor group.**
25. **Repeat steps 19-21** to **add Manager01 to the Manager group.**
26. **Repeat steps 19-21** to **add HRUser01 to the HumanResources group.**

27. **Make a screen capture** of the Active Directory window, **paste** it into a text document, and **submit** it as a deliverable for this lab.

> **Note:**
> To capture the screen, **press** the **Ctrl** and **PrtSc** keys together, and then **use Ctrl + V** to paste the image into a Word or other word processor document.

28. **Close** the **Active Directory window**.

> **Note:**
> The next steps will create a series of folders on the TargetWindows01 computer and then assign custom permission rights to each.

29. **Double-click** the **My Computer icon** on the TargetWindows01 desktop.
30. **Double-click** the **Local Disk (C:) icon**.
31. **Click File** in the toolbar, **click New,** and **select Folder** from the menu.
32. **Type ERPdocuments** to create a new folder.
33. **Right-click** the **C:\ERPdocuments folder**, and **select Sharing and Security** from the context menu.
34. In the **ERPdocuments Properties** dialog box, **click** the **Security tab**.
35. **Click** the **Advanced button**.
36. **Click** the **Allow inheritable permissions from the parent to propagate to this object and all child objects checkbox** to remove the check.
37. **Click** the **Remove button** in the Security dialog box to set custom security parameters for this folder.

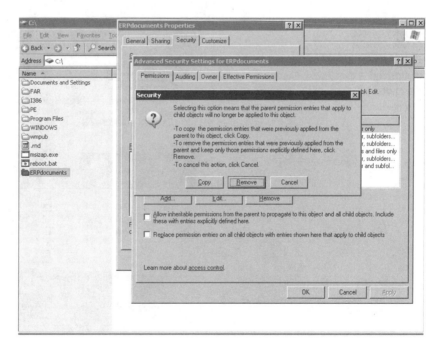

FIGURE 3.13

Remove inheritable permissions from a folder

By taking this step, you will be able to apply specific security groups to any new folders created under the ERPdocument folder.

38. **Click OK** to close the Advanced Security Settings for ERPdocuments dialog box.

39. On the Security tab of the ERPdocument Properties dialog box, **click** the **Add button.**

40. **Type Shopfloor; Manager; HumanResources** (the three new groups you created).

FIGURE 3.14

Adding security groups
to a folder

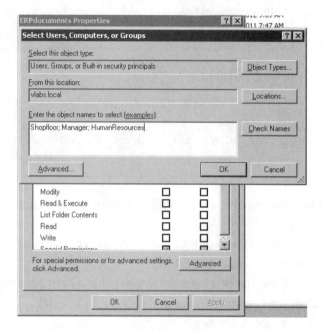

41. **Verify** that all three groups have been added to the Group or user names box in the ERPdocuments Properties dialog box, and **click OK.**

FIGURE 3.15

Three new security
groups added to
the folder

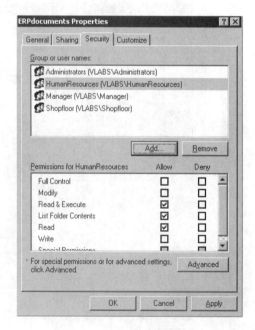

42. **Double-click** the **ERPdocuments folder**.

43. **Click File** in the toolbar, **click New**, and **select Folder** from the menu.

44. **Type HRfiles** to create a new folder for shared HumanResources (HR) user files.

45. **Click File** in the toolbar, **click New**, and **select Folder** from the menu.

46. **Type SFfiles** to create a new folder for shared Shopfloor (SF) user files.

47. **Click File** in the toolbar, **click New**, and **select Folder** from the menu.

48. **Type MGRfiles** to create a new folder for shared Manager (MGR) user files.

49. **Right-click** the **C:\ERPdocuments\HRfiles folder**, and **select Sharing and Security** from the context menu.

50. In the **HRfiles Properties** dialog box, **click** the **Security tab**.

51. **Click** the **Add button** to open the Select Users, Computers, or Group dialog box.

52. **Type HumanResources** and **click OK** to allow access to members of the HumanResources security group, including the new user named HRUser 01.

53. **Repeat steps 49-52** to add the **Shopfloor** security group to access the **SFfiles folder**.

54. **Repeat steps 49-52** to add the **Manager** security group to access both the **MGRfiles folder** and the **HRfiles folder**.

> **Note:**
> The next steps will modify permission rights on the TargetWindows01 server to allow these new users to access the server remotely.

55. **Click Start > Run** and **type gpedit.msc** in the dialog box.

56. **Click OK** to open the Group Policy Object Editor.

57. Navigate to the User Rights Assignment folder. **Click Computer Configuration**, **click Windows Settings**, **click Security Settings**, **click Local Policies**, and then **click User Rights Assignment**.

FIGURE 3.16

Group Policy Object Editor

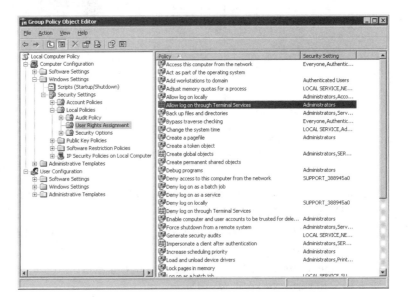

3

Enable Windows Active Directory and User Access Controls

58. **Double-click Allow log on through Terminal Services** in the right pane.
59. **Click** the **Add User or Group button** to open the Select Users, Computers, or Groups dialog box.
60. **Type Domain Users** in the **Enter the object names to select box** and **click Check Names** to allow Active Directory to verify the spelling.

FIGURE 3.17

Adding the Domain Users group to the Terminal Services policy

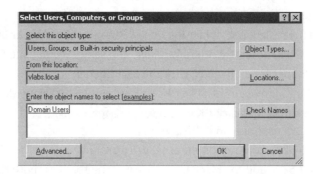

Domain Users is a "catch-all" group that includes all security groups found on the domain (in this case, the VLABS domain). You could also enter individual users or groups in this dialog box, but this is a more efficient method.

61. **Click OK twice** to save the changes and exit the dialog box.
62. **Double-click** the **Active Directory Users and Computers icon** on the desktop.
63. **Click** the **Builtin folder** in the left pane, and then **double-click Remote Desktop Users** in the right pane.

FIGURE 3.18

Selecting a Builtin group

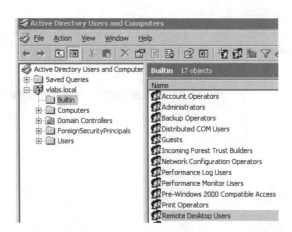

The Builtin group, including the Remote Desktop Users security group, is created as a part of the Active Directory service.

64. In the Remote Desktop Users Properties dialog box, **click** the **Members tab** and then **click** the **Add button** to add new users.
65. **Type Domain Users** in the **Enter the object names to select box** and **click Check Names** to allow Active Directory to verify the spelling of the group.
66. **Click OK twice** to save the changes and exit the Remote Desktop Users dialog box.
67. **Close** the **Active Directory Users and Computers window**.

68. **Click Start > Log Off** to disconnect your Administrator access to the TargetWindows01 server. Confirm your intent to log off when prompted. You will return to the vWorkstation desktop.

> **Note:**
> The next steps will test that the new users can access the TargetWindows01 server and save a file to the new folders you created in the previous steps.

69. **Double-click** the **TargetWindows01.rdp file** to open the Windows Server.
70. **Log on** to the **TargetWindows01 VM** server with the SFUser01 credentials:
    - User name: **SFUser01**
    - Password: **ISS316Security**
    - Log on to: **VLABS**

FIGURE 3.19

Logging on to TargetWindows01 Server as SFUser01

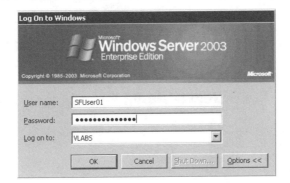

71. **Click OK** in the Connect to Server dialog box to start the FileZilla Server application.
72. **Close** the **FileZilla Server application**.
73. **Click Start > All Programs > Accessories** and then **double-click Notepad**.
    You will create a new file to save in the new folders you created on the server.
74. In the Notepad, **click File > Save as** to open the Save as dialog box.
75. **Name** the file **SFUser01** and **select Text Documents (*.txt)** from the Save as type drop-down menu. **Save** the file to the SFiles folder (**My Computer > Local Disk (C:) > ERPdocuments/SFfiles**).
76. In the Notepad, **click File > Save as** to open the Save as dialog box.
77. Attempt to **save** the same document to the HRfiles folder (**My Computer > Local Disk (C:) > ERPdocuments/HRfiles**).

    If the logged on user (SFUser01) does not have permission to write to a particular folder (HRfiles), you will see an error message.

FIGURE 3.20

Save As error message

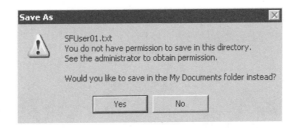

78. **Make a screen capture** of the error message and **paste** it into the text document.

> ▶ **Note:**
>
> To capture the screen, **press** the **Ctrl** and **PrtSc** keys together, and then **use Ctrl + V** to paste the image into a Word or other word processor document.

79. **Name** the file **SFUser01_error.txt** and **save** it in the SFfiles folder (**My Computer > Local Disk (C:) > ERPdocuments/SFfiles**).

80. **Make a screen capture** of the SFfiles folder showing the two files you saved and **paste** it into the text document and **submit** it to your instructor as a deliverable.

81. **Close Notepad**.

FIGURE 3.21

Saved text documents in the SFfiles folder

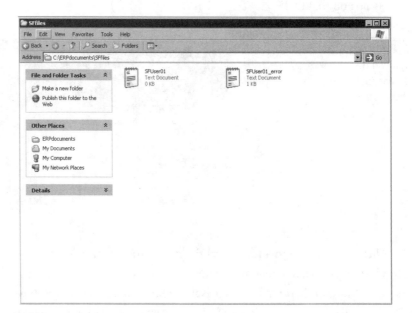

82. **Click Start > Log Off** to return to the vWorkstation.

83. **Repeat steps 69-82** using the **HRUser01** user account. Attempt to **save the text document** to the HRfiles folder (**My Computer > Local Disk (C:) > ERPdocuments/HRfiles**) and the MGRfiles folder (**My Computer > Local Disk (C:) > ERPdocuments/MGRfiles**).

84. **Repeat steps 69-82** using the **Manager01** user account. Attempt to **save the text document** to the HRfiles folder (**My Computer > Local Disk (C:) > ERPdocuments/HRfiles**), the MGRfiles folder (**My Computer > Local Disk (C:) > ERPdocuments/MGRfiles**), and the SFfiles folder (**My Computer > Local Disk (C:) > ERPdocuments/SFfiles**).

85. **Close** the **ISSA_VM Server Farm_RDP** window.

Evaluation Criteria and Rubrics

The following are the evaluation criteria and rubrics for Lab #3 that the students must perform:

1. Was the student able to design a Windows Active Directory and user access control framework? – [**20%**]

2. Was the student able to create a new Windows Active Directory domain controller definition? – [**20%**]

3. Was the student able to evaluate existing user and group permission rights in Active Directory user accounts and their workstations? – [**20%**]

4. Was the student able to create new Windows Active Directory users and groups with custom permission rights for user accounts and folders? – [**20%**]

5. Was the student able to create and verify access control lists to protect objects and folders from unauthorized access? – [**20%**]

LAB #3 – ASSESSMENT WORKSHEET

Enable Windows Active Directory and User Access Controls

Course Name and Number:

_____

Student Name:

_____

Instructor Name:

_____

Lab Due Date:

_____

Overview

This lab provided students with the hands-on skills needed to create a new Active Directory domain in Windows Server 2003 and demonstrated how to configure a centralized authentication and policy definition for access controls. The Active Directory users and workstation plug-ins were used to create users, groups, and configure role-based access permissions and controls on objects and folders in a Windows Server 2003 Active Directory system.

Lab Assessment Questions & Answers

1. What are the three fundamental elements of an effective access control solution for information systems?

_____

_____

_____

_____

2. What two access controls can be set up for Windows Server 2003 folders and authentication?

_____

_____

_____

_____

3. If you can browse a file on a Windows network share, but are not able to copy it or modify it, what type of access controls and permissions are probably configured? What type of access control would best describe this access control situation?

_____

_____

_____

_____

4. What is the mechanism on a Windows server where you can administer granular policies and permissions on a Windows network using role-based access?

_____

_____

_____

_____

5. What is two-factor authentication, and why is it an effective access control technique?

_____

_____

_____

_____

6. Relate how Windows Server 2008 R2 Active Directory and the configuration of access controls achieve CIA for departmental LANs, departmental folders, and data.

_____

_____

_____

_____

_____

_____

_____

7. Is it a good practice to include the account or user name in the password? Why or why not?

_____

_____

_____

_____

8. Can a user who is defined in the Active Directory access a shared drive if that user is not part of the domain?

_____

_____

_____

_____

9. Does Windows Server 2003 require a user's logon/password credentials prior to accessing shared drives?

_____

_____

_____

_____

10. When granting access to LAN systems for guests (i.e., auditors, consultants, third-party individuals, etc.), what security controls do you recommend be implemented to maximize CIA of production systems and data?

_____

_____

_____

_____

_____

_____

_____

_____

_____

Configure Group Policy Objects and Microsoft® Baseline Security Analyzer (MBSA)

Introduction

In this lab, you will use group policy objects to create a minimum password length password policy and link it to the newly created domain from the previous lab. You will also run the free Microsoft® Baseline Security Analyzer (MBSA) to assess the security state of the Targetw2k8a server and capture the results of that scan.

Learning Objectives

Upon completing this lab, you will be able to perform the following:

- Define Active Directory group policy objects (GPO) in Windows 2008 R2 Server
- Deploy GPOs to domain workstations within Windows 2008 R2 Server
- Configure logon credentials and specify password requirements and parameters for domain workstations within Windows 2008 R2 Server
- Use Microsoft® Baseline Security Analyzer (MBSA) to security baseline a Windows 2008 R2 Server and Windows XP Professional Workstation
- Enable automatic and online security updating and patching from Microsoft® Web servers via the Internet for Windows 2008 R2 Server and Windows XP Professional Workstation

TOOLS AND SOFTWARE USED	
NAME	**MORE INFORMATION**
Microsoft® Baseline Security Analyzer (MBSA)	http://www.microsoft.com/download/en/details.aspx?id=7558#overview

Deliverables

Upon completion of this lab, you are required to provide the following deliverables to your instructor:

1. Soft copy of your GPO report for the GPO created in this lab (in HTML format);
2. A text document that contains the results of the MBSA scan;
3. Lab Assessment Questions & Answers for Lab #4.

Hands-On Steps

1. This lab begins at the student landing vWorkstation virtual machine desktop of the VSCL, as shown here.

FIGURE 4.1

"Student Landing" VSCL workstation

2. **Double-click** the **ISSA_VM Server Farm_RDP icon** on the desktop. This folder contains links to the virtual servers in this lab environment.
3. **Double-click** the **Targetw2k8a.rdp file** to open the Windows Server.

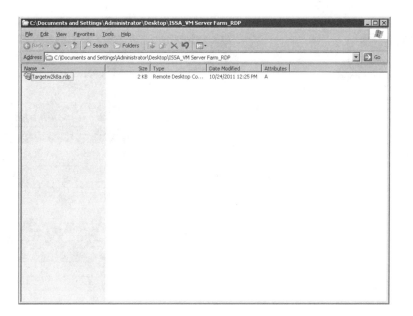

FIGURE 4.2

Open a remote desktop connection to the Targetw2k8a server

4. **Click OK** in the Remote Desktop Connection Security Warning alert to proceed.

FIGURE 4.3

Remote Desktop
Connection Security
Warning alert

5. **Double-click** the **vlabs\Administrator icon** on the Windows Server splash screen.
6. **Log on** to the **Targetw2k8a VM** server with the following credentials:
   - User name: **Administrator**
   - Password: **ISS316Security**

Note:
The next steps will use Group Policy Management Editor to review the existing password policies on the Targetw2k8a server.

7. **Click Start > Administrative Tools** and select **Group Policy Management** to open the group policy management console.

FIGURE 4.4

The Group Policy
Management console

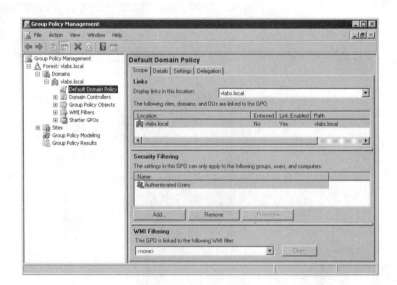

8. **Navigate** to the PasswordGPO folder. **Click Group Policy Objects** in the left pane.

9. **Right-click PasswordGPO** and select **Edit** from the context menu.

10. In the Group Policy Management Editor, navigate to the Password Policy folder. **Click** the **Policies folder** in the left pane, **click** the **Windows Settings folder, click** the **Security Settings folder, click** the **Account Policies folder,** and **click Password Policy.**

The Group Policy
Management Editor

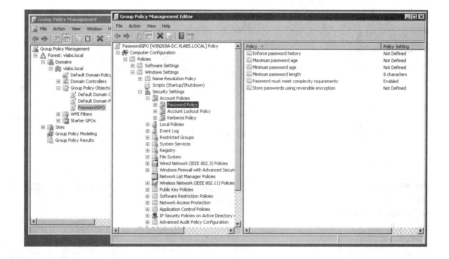

11. In the right pane, notice that the "Password must meet complexity requirements" policy is enabled. **Double-click Password must meet complexity requirements** to explore this policy.

12. **Click** the **Explain tab** and read the description for this policy. In particular, notice the minimum requirements for passwords in the center of the window.

The Explain tab

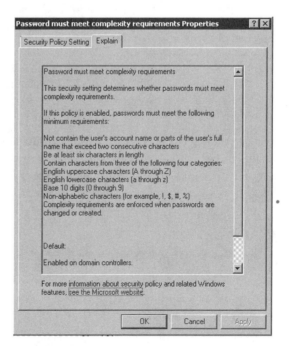

13. **Click OK** to close the window without making changes.

14. **Double-click Minimum Password Length t**o explore this policy. Notice that it currently requires that passwords be 8 characters long.

15. **Click** the **Explain tab** and read the description for this policy. In particular, notice the default settings in the center of the window.

16. **Click OK** to close the window without making changes.

17. Close the Group Policy Management Editor.

> **Note:**
> The next steps will use Group Policy Management Editor to link an existing group policy to the vlabs domain.

18. In the Group Policy Management console, **right-click vlabs.local** (the network domain) in the left pane and **select Link an Existing GPO** from the context menu.

FIGURE 4.7

Viewing linked group policy objects

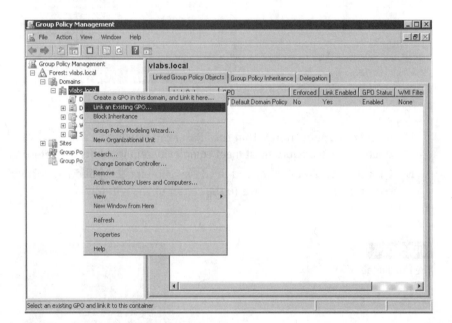

The Select GPO dialog box opens with a list of group policy objects (GPO) that are available to link to this domain.

19. **Click PasswordGPO** to select the policy that you reviewed in the previous steps.

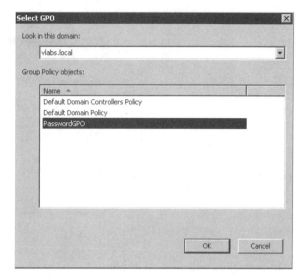

FIGURE 4.8

Linking an existing GPO
to a domain

20. **Click OK** to close the dialog box and apply the changes.

> **Note:**
> The next steps will create and save a GPO report. You will need this file as a deliverable for this lab.

21. In the Group Policy Management console, **right-click PasswordGPO** in the left pane and select Save
    Report from the context menu.

FIGURE 4.9

Saving a GPO report

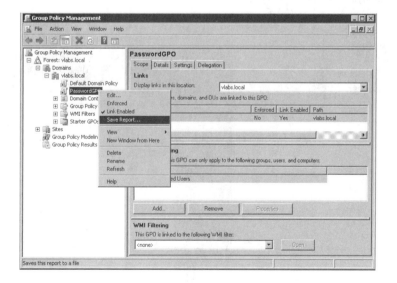

22. **Name** the file **PasswordGPO** and **select HTML File** from the Save as type drop-down menu. **Save** the file to the Targetw2k8a desktop.

FIGURE 4.10

Saving the PasswordGPO report

23. Close the Group Policy Management window.
24. **Double-click** the **PasswordGPO.html file** on the Targetw2k8a desktop to view the report in a Web browser.
25. **Close the browser window** and use the **File Transfer button** to submit the PasswordGPO.html file as a lab deliverable.

> **Note:**
> The next steps will use the Microsoft® Baseline Security Analyzer to perform a baseline security scan on the Targetw2k8a server. You will need this scan as a deliverable for this lab.

26. **Double-click** the **Microsoft® Baseline Security Analyzer 2.2 icon** on the Targetw2k8a desktop to launch the application.

FIGURE 4.11

Microsoft® Baseline Security Analyzer

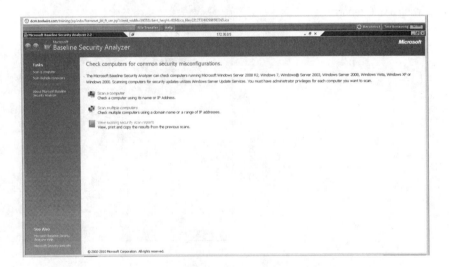

27. **Click Scan a computer** to begin the security scan.

28. **Click** the **Check for security updates** checkbox to remove the check.

    The Targetw2k8a server does not have direct Internet access, which is required to perform this check for updates. If you were running this scan on a computer with Internet access, leave this option selected.

FIGURE 4.12

Setting scan options

29. **Click** the **Start Scan button**.

30. When the scan is complete, **click Copy to clipboard** to save the output to the Windows clipboard.

FIGURE 4.13

Copying the scan results

31. **Minimize** the **Targetw2k8a window** and **paste** the clipboard contents into a new text editor or word processor file.

 Note:
You can create a text document using the Notepad application (Start > Programs > Accessories > Notepad) found on the vWorkstation.

32. **Save** the file as **Lab #4 MBSA Scan** to the Security_Strategies folder **(My Computer > Local Disk (C:) > Security_Strategies)**.

33. Use the **File Transfer button** and **submit** the Lab #4 MBSA Scan file as a lab deliverable.

34. **Maximize** the **Targetw2k8a** window and **close** the **Microsoft® Baseline Security Analyzer.**

35. **Close** the **Targetw2k8a** window.

36. **Close** the **ISSA_VM Server Farm_RDP folder.**

Evaluation Criteria and Rubrics

The following are the evaluation criteria and rubrics for Lab #4 that the students must perform:

1. Was the student able to define Active Directory group policy objects (GPO) in Windows 2008 R2 Server? – [**20%**]

2. Was the student able to deploy GPOs to domain workstations within Windows 2008 R2 Server? – [**20%**]

3. Was the student able to configure logon credentials and specify password requirements and parameters for domain workstations within Windows 2008 R2 Server? – [**20%**]

4. Was the student able to use Microsoft® Baseline Security Analyzer (MBSA) to security baseline a Windows 2008 R2 Server and Windows XP Professional Workstation? – [**20%**]

5. Was the student able to facilitate the automatic and online security updating and patching from Microsoft® Web servers via the Internet for Windows 2008 R2 Server and Windows XP Professional Workstation? – [**20%**]

LAB #4 – ASSESSMENT WORKSHEET

Configure Group Policy Objects and Microsoft® Baseline Security Analyzer (MBSA)

Course Name and Number:
_____

Student Name:
_____

Instructor Name:
_____

Lab Due Date:
_____

Overview

In this lab, you used group policy objects to create a minimum password length password policy and link it to the newly created domain from the previous lab. You also ran the Microsoft® Baseline Security Analyzer (MBSA) and reviewed the results of the MBSA scan.

Lab Assessment Questions & Answers

1. Define why change control management is relevant to security operations in an organization.

_____

_____

_____

_____

2. What type of access control system uses security labels?

_____

_____

_____

_____

3. Describe two options you would enable in a Windows Domain password policy.

_____

_____

_____

_____

4. Where would patch management and software updates fall under in security operations and management?

_____

_____

_____

_____

5. Is there a setting in your GPO to specify how many logon attempts will lock out an account? Name two parameters that you can set to enhance the access control to the system.

_____

_____

_____

_____

6. What are some password policy parameter options you can define for GPOs that can enhance the CIA for system access?

_____

_____

_____

_____

7. What sources could you use as a source to perform the MBSA security state?

_____

_____

_____

_____

8. What does WSUS stand for, and what does it do?

_____

_____

_____

_____

9. What is the difference between MBSA and Microsoft® Update?

_____

_____

_____

_____

10. What are some of the options that you can exercise when using the MBSA tool?

_____

_____

_____

_____

Perform Protocol Capture and Analysis Using Wireshark and NetWitness Investigator

Introduction

In this lab, you will use FileZilla and the Tftpd32 application to transfer files between machines in this lab. You will capture data using Wireshark, a packet capture and protocol analysis tool. Following a successful packet capture, you will use NetWitness Investigator, a free tool that provides security practitioners with a means of analyzing that full packet capture.

Learning Objectives

Upon completing this lab, you will be able to:

- Use Wireshark and NetWitness Investigator as a packet capture and protocol analysis tool
- Capture live IP, ICMP, TCP, and UDP traffic using Telnet, FTP, TFTP, and SSH sessions
- Examine captured packet traces to view cleartext and ciphertext
- Analyze the packet capture data in both Wireshark and NetWitness Investigator and be able to identify the difference between UDP and TCP sessions
- Identify common network-related protocols used for client-server communications, network management, and network security

TOOLS AND SOFTWARE	
NAME	**MORE INFORMATION**
FileZilla Server and FileZilla Client	http://filezilla-project.org/
NetWitness Investigator	http://www.emc.com/security/rsa-netwitness.htm
PuTTY	http://www.chiark.greenend.org.uk/~sgtatham/putty/
Tftpd32	http://tftpd32.jounin.net/
Wireshark	http://www.wireshark.org/

Deliverables

Upon completion of this lab, you are required to provide the following deliverables to your instructor:

1. Wireshark Protocol Capture File;
2. Text document with a NetWitness Investigator screenshot of the imported *.pcap file;
3. Lab Assessment Questions & Answers for Lab #5.

Hands-On Steps

1. This lab begins at the student landing vWorkstation virtual machine desktop of the VSCL, as
   shown here.

> **Note:**
> The next steps log on to the Windows and Linux virtual servers. You will use both of these servers during
> this lab.

2. **Double-click** the **ISSA_VM Server Farm_RDP icon** on the desktop. This folder contains links to the virtual
   servers in this lab environment.
3. **Double-click** the **TargetWindows01.rdp file** to open the Windows Server.

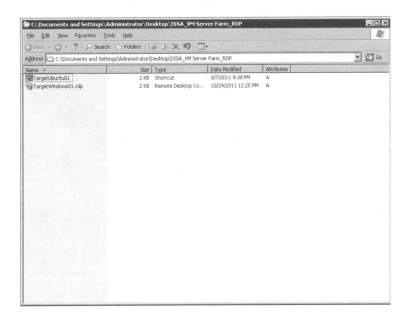

4. **Log on** to the **TargetWindows01 VM** server with the following credentials:
   - User name: **Administrator**
   - Password: **ISS316Security**

5. **Click OK** in the Connect to Server dialog box to start the FileZilla Server application.

   This dialog box loads automatically when the Windows server starts, with the address and password already filled in.

FIGURE 5.3

Connect to Server dialog box

6. **Minimize** the **FileZilla Server application**.
7. **Minimize** the **TargetWindows01 window**.
8. In the **ISSA_VM Server Farm_RDP folder, double-click** the **TargetUbuntu01 icon** to open the lab's Linux Server.
9. **Log in** to the **TargetUbuntu01 VM** server with the following credentials:
   - User name: **student**
   - Password: **ISS316Security**

FIGURE 5.4

Connect to TargetUbuntu01 server

10. **Minimize** the **TargetUbuntu01 window** to return to the vWorkstation desktop.
11. **Close the ISSA_VM Server Farm_RDP folder.**

> **Note:**
> The next steps will use the Wireshark application to capture data packets for later analysis.

12. **Double-click** the **Wireshark icon** on the desktop to start that application.

The Wireshark window

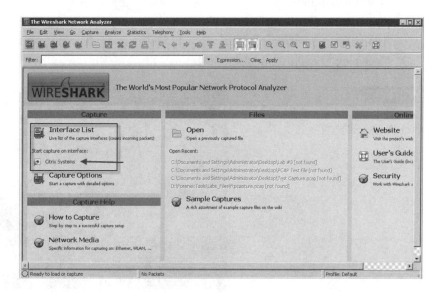

13. **Click** the **Citrix Systems link** in the Interface List section of the application window.

Wireshark immediately begins capturing data from the vWorkstation desktop (172.30.0.2), the
TargetWindows01 server (172.30.0.8), and the TargetUbuntu01 server (172.30.0.4).

Data from the Wireshark
capture

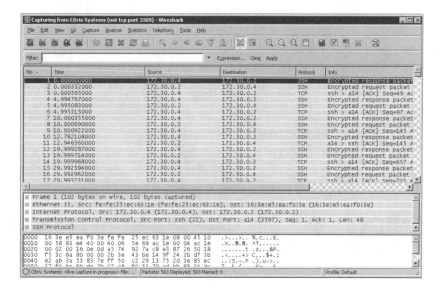

14. **Minimize** the **Wireshark application**.

> **Note:**
> The next steps will use the Windows Command Prompt to make sure that the destination IP addresses you will
> use in this lab are available. You will then use the PuTTY application to establish a Telnet or SSH connection to
> those same IP addresses. These steps will gather more data for Wireshark to capture.

15. From the vWorkstation desktop, **click** the **Windows Start button**.

16. **Select Run** from the menu.

17. **Type cmd** in the dialog box and **click OK**.

18. In the Windows Command Prompt window, ping the IP address for the vWorkstation desktop. **Type ping 172.30.0.2** and **press Enter**.

```
C:\WINDOWS\system32\cmd.exe
Microsoft Windows [Version 5.2.3790]
(C) Copyright 1985-2003 Microsoft Corp.

C:\Documents and Settings\Administrator>ping 172.30.0.2

Pinging 172.30.0.2 with 32 bytes of data:

Reply from 172.30.0.2: bytes=32 time<1ms TTL=128
Reply from 172.30.0.2: bytes=32 time<1ms TTL=128
Reply from 172.30.0.2: bytes=32 time<1ms TTL=128
Reply from 172.30.0.2: bytes=32 time<1ms TTL=128

Ping statistics for 172.30.0.2:
    Packets: Sent = 4, Received = 4, Lost = 0 (0% loss),
Approximate round trip times in milli-seconds:
    Minimum = 0ms, Maximum = 0ms, Average = 0ms

C:\Documents and Settings\Administrator>_
```

19. **Repeat step 18** for each of the following IP addresses:
    - LAN Switch 1: **172.16.8.5**
    - LAN Switch 2: **172.16.20.5**
    - TargetWindows01: **172.30.0.8**
    - TargetUbuntu01: **172.30.0.4**
    - Indy: **172.17.0.2**
    - Tampa: **172.16.0.2**
    - WestCovina: **172.19.0.2**

    Replies indicate that the IP address is available. Alert your instructor if you do not receive a reply from a particular IP address.

20. **Close** the **Windows Command Prompt window**.

21. **Double-click** the **PuTTY icon** on the desktop to start the PuTTY application.

22. In the PuTTY application window, type the IP address for LAN Switch 1, **172.16.8.5. Select** the **Telnet radio button** and **click** the **Open** button to start the connection.

23. PuTTY will launch a terminal console window. At the login prompt, **type** the following credentials:
    * User name: **cisco**
    * Password: **cisco**

FIGURE 5.9

PuTTY terminal console
window

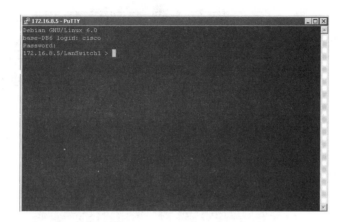

24. In the terminal console window, **type quit** to close the terminal console.
25. **Repeat steps 21-24** for each of the following IP addresses:
    * Indy: **172.17.0.2**
    * Tampa: **172.16.0.2**
26. **Double-click** the **PuTTY icon** on the desktop to start the PuTTY application.
27. In the PuTTY application window, **type** the IP address for LAN Switch 2, **172.16.20.5. Select** the **SSH radio button** and **click** the **Open button** to start the connection.
28. PuTTY will launch a terminal console window. At the login prompt, **type** the following credentials:
    * User name: **cisco**
    * Password: **cisco**
29. In the terminal console window, **type quit** to close the terminal console.
30. **Repeat steps 26-29** for each of the following IP addresses:
    * TargetUbuntu01: **172.30.0.4**
    * WestCovina: **172.19.0.2**

> **Note:**
> The next steps will gather additional packet data by using the Tftpd32 application and FileZilla to send several small files between clients and servers on the various machines.

31. **Double-click** the **Tftpd32_SE Admin icon** on the vWorkstation desktop to launch the application.

    The Tftpd32_SE application uses the TFTP (Trivial File Transfer Protocol) to send (put) or receive (get) files between computers.

FIGURE 5.10

The Tftpd32 application

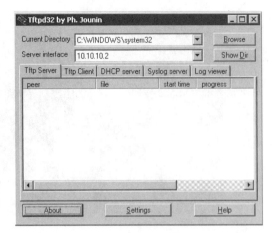

32. When the application window launches, **click** the **Tftp Client tab** to set up the TargetWindows01 virtual server as the Tftp client (or receiving computer).

33. On the Tftp Client tab, **type or select** the following information and click the **Put button**:
    * Host: **172.30.0.8** (TargetWindows01)
    * Port: **69**
    * Local File: **C:\Documents and Settings\Administrator\My Documents\PCAP Test File**
    * Remote file: **test.txt**
    * Block Size: **Default**

FIGURE 5.11

Tftp a file to the TargetWindows01 server

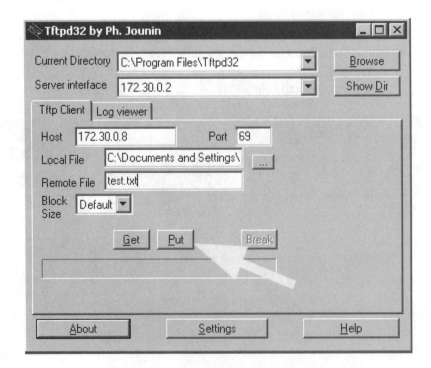

34. Maximize the **TargetWindows01 window** and **verify** that the FileZilla application is running.

The FileZilla application
window

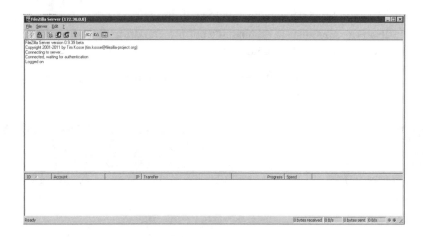

If the FileZilla application is not running, you can open it by **double-clicking** on the **FileZilla Server Interface icon** on the TargetWindows01 desktop.

35. Minimize the **TargetWindows01 desktop**.

36. Double-click the **FileZilla icon** on the vWorkstation desktop.

37. Type the following login credentials in the address boxes at the top of the application window that opens to connect to the FileZilla Server on the TargetWindows01 server:

- Host: **172.30.0.8**
- User name: **student**
- Password: **ISS316Security**
- Port: **21**

38. Click the **Quickconnect button** to connect to the FileZilla Server.

Connecting to
FileZilla Server on
TargetWindows01 using
the FileZilla Client

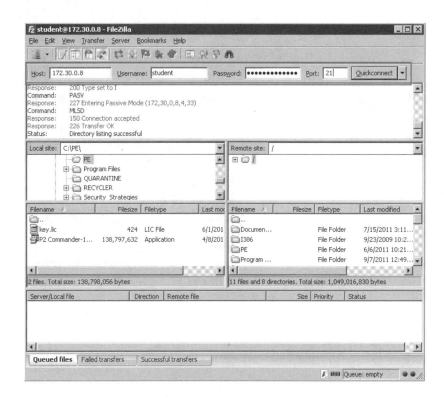

39. **Navigate** to the **C:\Security_Strategies\ISSA_TOOLS\Documentation folder** in the Local site (vWorkstation) directory.

40. **Select** the **AnyConnect_adminguide.pdf file**.

41. **Drag** the **AnyConnect_adminguide.pdf file** and **drop** it into the **root directory folder** in the Remote site (TargetWindows01) pane.

The status responses in the area below the connection information indicate whether or not the file transfer was successful.

FIGURE 5.14

Successful FTP from vWorkstation to TargetWindows01

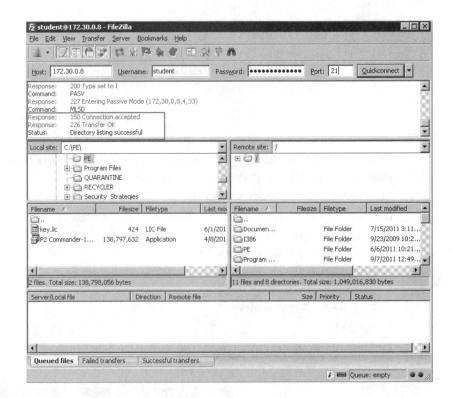

42. **Maximize** the **TargetWindows01 desktop** and **verify** that the file was transferred.

FIGURE 5.15

Successful FTP transfer of the AnyConnect_adminguide.pdf file

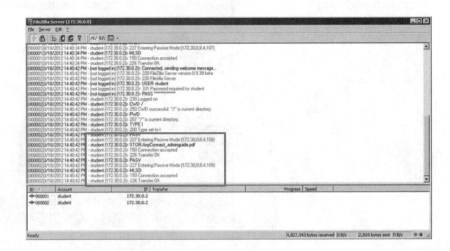

43. **Close** the **FileZilla Server window**.

44. **Double-click** the **Tftpd32_SE Admin icon** on the TargetWindows01 desktop.

45. When the application window launches, **click** the **Tftp Client tab** to set up the TargetWindows01 server as the Tftp client (or receiving computer).

46. **Minimize** the **TargetWindows01 window** to return to the vWorkstation desktop.

47. **Double-click** the **Tftpd32_SE Admin icon** and **click** the **Tftp Server tab** to establish the vWorkstation as the Tftp server (or sending computer).

48. **Maximize** the **TargetWindows01 window** to return to the TargetWindows01 desktop.

49. On the Tftp Server tab, **type or select** the following information and click the **Put button**:
    - Host: **172.30.0.2** (vWorkstation)
    - Port: **69**
    - Local File: **C:\AnyConnect_adminguide.pdf**
    - Block Size: **Default**

    This is the same file that you transferred using FileZilla earlier in this lab. The status responses in the area below the connection information indicate whether or not the file transfer was successful.

50. **Close** the **Tftpd32 application**.

51. **Minimize** the **TargetWindows01 window** to return to the vWorkstation desktop.

52. **Close** the **Tftpd32 application** on the vWorkstation desktop.

> **Note:**
> The next steps will stop the data capture that Wireshark has been collecting, and save a .pcap file for analysis later in this lab. You will need this file as a deliverable for this lab.

53. **Maximize** the **Wireshark application**, if necessary.

54. **Click** the **Stop icon** to stop the packet capture process.

55. **Click** the **Save icon** to save the packet capture. When the "Wireshark: Save file as" dialog box opens, **name** the file **Lab #5** and **select Wireshark/tcpdump…libpcap [*.pcap, *.cap]** from the "Save as type" menu. **Save** the file to the Security_Strategies folder (**My Computer > Local Disk (C:) > Security_Strategies**).

56. Use the **File Transfer button** to **download** the **Lab #5.pcap file** to your local computer and **submit** it as part of your deliverables.

57. **Close** the **Wireshark application**.

> **Note:**
> The next steps will use NetWitness Investigator to analyze the Wireshark packet capture you just saved. NetWitness Investigator allows you to look at and analyze packet capture data in context, so that you are able to act on any threats or problems quickly and easily. These steps show you how to build a NetWitness Investigator local collection, which you can use to analyze and submit your package capture data to your instructor as part of the lab deliverables.

58. **Double-click** the **NetWitness Investigator icon** on the vWorkstation desktop to start the application.

59. When the application window launches, **click Collection** in the toolbar and **select New Local Collection**.

60. In the New Local Collection dialog box, **name** the collection **Lab #5** and save it to the default location by **clicking OK**.

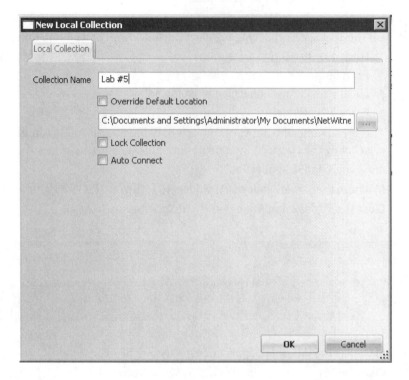

FIGURE 5.16

New Local Collection
dialog box

A new collection named Lab #5 will appear at the bottom of the collection list in the left pane of the application window.

61. **Double-click** on the new **Lab #5** collection to change the status to **Ready**.

62. **Right-click** on the new **Lab #5** collection and **select Import Packets** from the context menu.

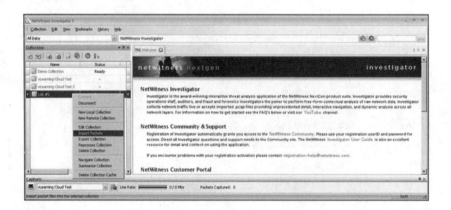

FIGURE 5.17

Importing a PCAP
file into NetWitness
Investigator

63. In the Open dialog box, **navigate** to the Security_Strategies folder (**My Computer > Local Disk (C:) > Security_Strategies**) and **select** the **Lab #5.pcap file**. **Click Open** to import the file.

FIGURE 5.18

Opening the Lab #5.
pcap file

64. **Double-click** the new **Lab #5** collection to review the information captured by Wireshark.

FIGURE 5.19

Summary information

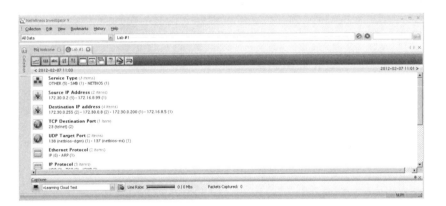

65. **Make a screen capture** of this screen and **paste** it into a new text document. **Submit** it to your instructor as a deliverable.

> **Note:**
> To capture the screen, **press** the **Ctrl** and **PrtSc** keys together, and then **use Ctrl + V** to paste the image into a Word or other word processor document.

66. **Close** the **NetWitness Investigator window**.

Evaluation Criteria and Rubrics

The following are the evaluation criteria and rubrics for Lab #5 that the students must perform:

1. Was the student able to use Wireshark and NetWitness Investigator as a packet capture and protocol analysis tool? – **[20%]**

2. Was the student able to capture live IP, ICMP, TCP, and UDP traffic using Telnet, FTP, TFTP, and SSH sessions and distinguish them? – **[20%]**

3. Was the student able to examine captured packet traces to view cleartext and ciphertext data? – **[20%]**

4. Was the student able to analyze the packet capture data in Wireshark or NetWitness Investigator? And was the student able to identify the difference between UDP and TCP sessions? – **[20%]**

5. Was the student able to identify common network-related protocols used for client-server communications, network management, and network security? – **[20%]**

LAB #5 – ASSESSMENT WORKSHEET

Perform Protocol Capture and Analysis Using Wireshark and NetWitness Investigator

Course Name and Number:

_____

Student Name:

_____

Instructor Name:

_____

Lab Due Date:

_____

Overview

One of the most important tools needed for information systems security practitioners is a packet capture and protocol analysis tool. Wireshark is a freeware tool providing basic packet capture and protocol decoding capabilities. NetWitness Investigator provides security practitioners with a deep packet inspection tool used for examining everything from the data link layer up to the application layer.

Lab Assessment Questions & Answers

1. What is the purpose of the address resolution protocol (ARP)?

_____

_____

_____

_____

2. What is the purpose of the dynamic host control protocol (DHCP)?

_____

_____

_____

_____

3. What was the DHCP allocated source IP host address for the "Student" VM and Target VM?

_____

_____

_____

_____

4. When you pinged the targeted IP host, what was the source IP address and destination IP address of the ICMP echo-request packet?

_____

_____

_____

_____

5. Did the targeted IP host respond to the ICMP echo-request packet with an ICMP echo-reply packet? If yes, how many ICMP echo-request packets were sent back to the IP source?

_____

_____

_____

_____

6. Find a TCP three-way handshake for a Telnet, FTP, or SSH session. What is the significance of the TCP three-way handshake?

_____

_____

_____

_____

7. What was the SEQ# of the initial SYN TCP packet and ACK# of the SYN ACK TCP packet?

_____

_____

_____

_____

8. During the instructor's Telnet session to LAN Switch 1 and LAN Switch 2, what was the captured terminal password for LAN Switch 1 and LAN Switch 2?

_____

_____

_____

_____

9. When the instructor used SSH to remotely access a Cisco router, were you able to see the terminal password? Why or why not?

_____

_____

_____

_____

10. What other IP packets are on the VLAN and Ethernet LAN segment? How can these other IP packets provide additional clues or information about the logical IP routing and IP addressing schema?

_____

_____

_____

_____

Perform Business Continuity Implementation Planning

Introduction

In this lab, you have been asked to begin the business continuity planning process for an e-commerce company, Online Goodies. You will review the key business functions and a prioritized list of impacted IT systems, applications, and data provided by your supervisor. You also will compare the components of the major documentation required by the business continuity planning process: risk analysis, business impact analysis, business continuity plan, disaster recovery plan, and the business continuity implementation plan.

This lab is a paper-based design lab and does not require use of the Virtual Security Cloud Lab (VSCL). To successfully complete the deliverables for this lab, you will need access to a text editor or word processor, such as Microsoft® Word. For some labs, you may also need access to a graphics line drawing application, such as Visio or PowerPoint.

> **Note:**
> If you don't have a word processor or graphics package, use OpenOffice on the student landing vWorkstation for your lab deliverables and to answer the lab assessment questions. To capture screenshots, **press Prt Sc > MSPAINT**, paste into a text document, and save the document in the Security_Strategies folder (**C:\Security_Strategies**) using the File Transfer function.

Learning Objectives and Outcomes

Upon completing this lab, you will be able to:

- Identify the major elements of a business continuity plan (BCP) and requirements for a fictitious organization
- Perform a high-level business impact analysis (BIA) and risk analysis (RA) for a fictitious organization
- Prioritize from the BIA and RA business functions and processes that must be part of the business continuity plan
- Craft a BCP plan outline that addresses the BIA and RA and business priorities
- Define the necessary BCP implementation planning steps that include testing, practice, and documentation maintenance of backup and recovery procedures

Deliverables

Upon completion of this lab, you are required to provide the following deliverables to your instructor:

1. Business Continuity Planning Lab #6;
2. Lab Assessment Questions & Answers for Lab #6.

Hands-On Steps

1. This lab begins with a request from your supervisor. As the newest member of the network administration team for a fictitious e-commerce company, Online Goodies, you will be required to begin the business continuity planning process, based on the information included in this lab. Your supervisor has already interviewed key personnel throughout the company and provides you with a list of the key business functions and processes for the company, and a prioritized list of the impacted IT systems.

FIGURE 6.1

Online Goodies' key
business functions
and processes

Key Business Functions and Processes

☐ E-commerce processes *(primary revenue source for the organization)*
☐ E-mail-based communications *(internal for business communications and external for customer service)*
☐ Telephone call center and online customer services *(enhanced e-customer service delivery with call center and self-service customer website)*
☐ Manufacturing and production line *(just-in-time inventory and distribution of products)*
☐ Production processes *(just-in-time manufacturing and integrated supply chain)*
☐ Quality control mechanisms *(maximize product quality)*
☐ Maintenance and support services *(keep production lines open)*
☐ Sales and sales administration *(inside sales, online sales, sales support, re-sellers and distributors, etc.)*
☐ Finance and accounting *(General ledger, A/R, A/P, payroll, benefits)*
☐ Research and development activities *(product development)*
☐ Human resources management *(employee services)*
☐ Information technology services and Internet connectivity *(supports e-commerce and e-business infrastructure)*
☐ Premises *(headquarters facility, branches, and administration office)*
☐ Marketing and public relations *(Internet marketing and branding)*

6

Perform Business Continuity
Implementation Planning

FIGURE 6.2

Online Goodies' prioritized list of impacted IT systems

BUSINESS FUNCTION OR PROCESS	PRIORITY	IT SYSTEMS, APPLICATIONS, AND DATA
E-mail-based communications	10	POP3, SMTP Mail Servers
Website and e-commerce website (Payroll for HR)	1	Web Server, e-Commerce Server (Manual Payroll Processing or External)
Telephone call center	3	VoIP Telephony Infrastructure
Customer service	4	Customer Server System/CRM
Manufacturing and production line	7	Automation System & Manufacturing
Production processes	8	Production Scheduling System
Quality control mechanisms	11	QC System
Maintenance and support services	13	Maintenance & Support System
Sales and sales administration	6	Sales Order Entry, Sales Support
Finance and accounting	9	GL, A/R, A/P Accounting System
Research and development activities	16	R&D System
Human resources management	14	HR, Employment, Benefits
Information technology services	2	7-Domains of Typical IT Infrastructure (Website/Internet/Online)
Internet connectivity & telephone service	5	Broadband Internet, VoIP System
Premises (Head Office and branches)	12	HQ LAN/VoIP/IT Infrastructure
Marketing and public relations	15	Marketing Analysis System

> **Note:**
> The next steps will guide you through the steps you will take to create the Business Continuity Planning Lab #6 deliverable for this lab.

2. From a computer workstation, **create** a new text document called **Business Continuity Planning Lab #6.**

   You will follow the steps in this lab as if you were part of the network administration team. You will be responsible for determining what to document in this deliverable.

3. In your text document, **describe** the difference between a risk analysis (RA), business impact analysis (BIA), business continuity plan (BCP), and a disaster recovery plan (DRP).

4. In your text document, **describe** your assessment of how this prioritization will impact the need for IT systems, applications, and data access.

5. Based on your knowledge of this topic, **order** the following topics according to the optimal sequence of events for completing a proper risk assessment and business impact analysis, and then **describe** your reasoning:

   - Prioritize the business' critical business functions and processes
   - Develop an information-gathering questionnaire
   - Assess the financial impact that a loss to critical business functions and processes will have on the business
   - Conduct interviews and one-on-one meetings with business leaders and departmental managers of critical business functions and processes
   - Identify the IT systems, applications, and data that support the critical business functions and processes
   - Align business drivers with key business functions and processes

6. In your text document, **define** the following key business continuity metrics that drive the overall business continuity plan:

   - Business risk analysis and business impact analysis prioritization of critical business functions and processes
   - Recovery time objectives (RTO) for the critical business functions and processes
   - Financial loss versus cost of recovery impact analysis

7. In your text document, **discuss** how to define the scope of the BCP and how that scope can be narrowed based on mission critical priorities and financial budgets.

8. In your text document, **discuss** how business asset replacement insurance can impact the cost and investment of business continuity solutions.

9. In your text document, **describe** the differences between the business continuity plan and the business continuity implementation plan, comparing the major components of each document.

10. **Submit** the **text document** to your instructor as a deliverable for this lab.

Evaluation Criteria and Rubrics

The following are the evaluation criteria and rubrics for Lab #6 that the students must perform:

1. Was the student able to identify the major elements of a business continuity plan (BCP) and requirements for a fictitious organization? – [**20%**]

2. Was the student able to perform a high-level business impact analysis (BIA) and risk analysis (RA) for a fictitious organization? – [**20%**]

3. Was the student able to prioritize from the BIA and RA business functions and processes that must be part of the business continuity plan? – [**20%**]

4. Was the student able to craft a BCP plan outline that addresses the BIA and RA and business priorities? – [**20%**]

5. Was the student able to define the necessary BCP implementation planning steps that include testing, practice, and documentation of backup and recovery procedures? – [**20%**]

LAB #6 – ASSESSMENT WORKSHEET

Perform Business Continuity Implementation Planning

Course Name and Number:
_____

Student Name:
_____

Instructor Name:
_____

Lab Due Date:
_____

Overview

In this lab, you were asked to begin the business continuity planning process for an e-commerce company, Online Goodies. You reviewed the key business functions and a prioritized list of impacted IT systems, applications, and data provided by your supervisor. You also compared the components of the major documentation required by the business continuity planning process: risk analysis, business impact analysis, business continuity plan, disaster recovery plan, and the business continuity implementation plan.

Lab Assessment Questions & Answers

1. What is the difference between a risk analysis (RA) and a business impact analysis (BIA)?

_____

_____

_____

_____

2. What is the difference between a disaster recovery plan (DRP) and a business continuity plan (BCP)?

_____

_____

_____

_____

3. Typically, a business continuity plan is also a compilation or collection of other plans. What other plans might a BCP and all supporting documents include?

_____

_____

_____

_____

4. Why is it important to have detailed backup and recovery steps within your disaster recovery plan (DRP)?

_____

_____

_____

_____

5. What is the purpose of a risk analysis? What is the purpose of a business impact analysis? Why are these an important first step in defining a BCP and DRP?

_____

_____

_____

_____

6. How does risk analysis (RA) relate to a business impact analysis for an organization?

_____

_____

_____

_____

7. Given the list of identified mission critical business functions and processes, what kind of company would you say this organization is, and what do you think are its most important business processes and functions?

_____

_____

_____

_____

8. Given the prioritization list provided for the organization's identified business functions and processes, write an assessment of how this prioritization will impact the need for IT systems, applications, and data access.

_____

_____

_____

_____

9. For the top five identified business functions and processes, what recovery time objective (RTO) would you recommend for this organization and why?

_____

_____

_____

_____

10. Why is payroll for employees and human resources also listed as a No. 1 business priority?

_____

_____

_____

_____

6

Perform Business Continuity
Implementation Planning

Relate Windows Encryption and Hashing to Confidentiality and Integrity

Introduction

In this lab, you will learn how hashing tools can be used to ensure message and file transfer integrity and how encryption can be used to maximize confidentiality. You will use both MD5 and SHA1, common hashing tools, on a sample file comparing the hash value when the sample file is modified or altered. You will also use Kleopatra (GPG4Win) to generate both a public and private key, and you will generate a secret key for encryption only.

Learning Objectives

Upon completing this lab, you will be able to:

- Apply the concepts of using common cryptographic and encryption techniques to ensure confidentiality
- Apply the concepts of hashing to ensure integrity of data transmission and data reception
- Identify the output of common cryptographic and hashing tools on transmitted data, and verify confidentiality and integrity
- Implement an MD5 sum or SHA1 hash on a data transmission or message to verify data transmission integrity
- Implement GPG for Windows to encrypt a data message to ensure confidentiality

TOOLS AND SOFTWARE	
NAME	**MORE INFORMATION**
FileZilla Server and FileZilla Client	http://filezilla-project.org/
GPG4Win	http://www.gpg4win.org/
Kleopatra	http://www.kde.org/applications/utilities/kleopatra/

Deliverables

Upon completion of this lab, you are required to provide the following deliverables to your instructor:

1. Your original encrypted file;
2. Your original decrypted file;
3. Screen capture of your successful decrypted message submitted in a text document;
4. Lab Assessment Questions & Answers for Lab #7.

Hands-On Steps

1. This lab begins at the student landing vWorkstation virtual machine desktop of the VSCL, as shown here.

FIGURE 7.1

"Student Landing" VSCL workstation

> **Note:**
> The next steps use Kleopatra, the certificate management component of GPG4Win, to create a set of keys, or certificates, to aid in encrypting and decrypting files later in this lab.

2. **Double-click** the **Kleopatra icon** on the desktop to open the Kleopatra component of the GPG4Win application.
3. **Click File** from the toolbar and **select New Certificate**.

FIGURE 7.2

Create a new certificate using Kleopatra

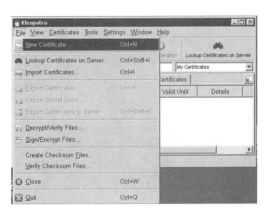

7

Relate Windows Encryption
and Hashing to Confidentiality
and Integrity

4. **Click** the **Create a personal OpenPGP key pair** option in the Certificate Creation Wizard.

5. Complete the Enter Details screen with the following information and **click Next** to continue:
   - Name: **Student01**
   - EMail: **student01@vlabsolutions.com**

FIGURE 7.3

Creating a new
certificate using
Kleopatra

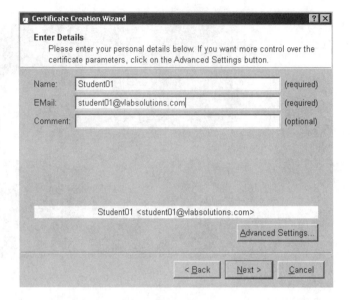

6. **Click** the **Show all details checkbox** to view the key type, strength, and usage of the certificate.

7. **Click** the **Create Key button**.

FIGURE 7.4

Reviewing certificate
parameters

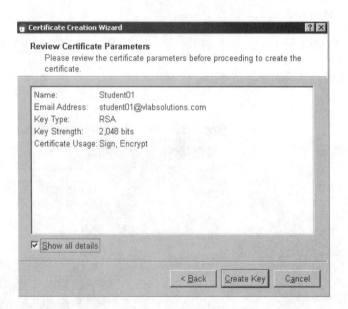

A pinentry (pin entry) dialog box will pop up to complete the creation of a key. You will enter a passphrase (password) to decrypt the file later.

8. In the pinentry dialog box, **type ISS316Security** and **click OK**.

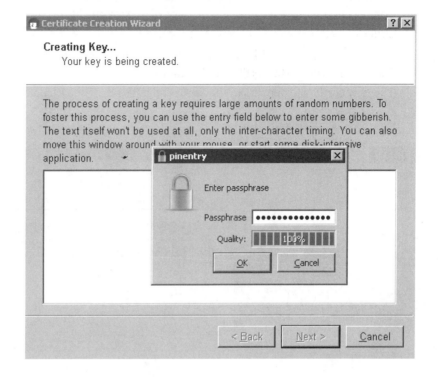

9. **Type ISS316Security** again when prompted to re-enter the passphrase. **Click OK** to generate the key.
10. **Click** the **Make a Backup of Your Key Pair button**.

Certificate Creation Wizard   [?][X]

Key Pair Successfully Created
   Your new key pair was created successfully. Please find details on the
   result and some suggested next steps below.

Result
   Certificate created successfully.
   Fingerprint: 10D42AC847B97D0D08D740E9BF05DC33B813B9D1

Next Steps
   Make a Backup Of Your Key Pair...
   Send Certificate By EMail...
   Upload Certificate To Directory Service...

                                           < Back   Finish

11. **Click** the **Save icon** in the Export Secret Certificate dialog box.

12. In the Save as dialog box, **name** the file **studentvm** and **select Secret Key Files [*.gpg, *.asc, *.p12, *pem, *.pgp]** from the "Save as type" menu. **Click OK** to save the file to the vWorkstation desktop.

13. **Click OK** to close the Export Secret Certificate dialog box.

14. **Click OK** to close the Certificate Export Finished dialog box.

15. **Click Finish** to close the Certificate Creation Wizard.

    The new certificate appears in the My Certificates tab of the Kleopatra application.

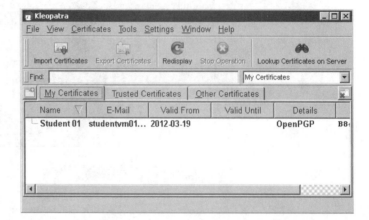

16. **Click** the **new certificate** you just created and **click** the **Export Certificates button** in the application's toolbar to save a public key.

17. In the Export Certificates dialog box, **name** the file **studentvm01_public** and **select OpenPGP Certificates [*.asc, *.gpg, *.pgp]** from the "Save as type" menu. **Click Save** to save the file to the vWorkstation desktop.

18. **Close** the **Kleopatra application.**

Note:

The next steps use Kleopatra, the certificate management component of GPG4Win, to create a set of keys on the TargetWindows01 desktop.

---

19. **Double-click** the **ISSA_VM Server Farm_RDP icon** on the desktop. This folder contains links to the virtual servers in this lab environment.

20. Double-click the **TargetWindows01.rdp file** to open the Windows Server.

FIGURE 7.8

Open a remote desktop
connection to the
TargetWindows01

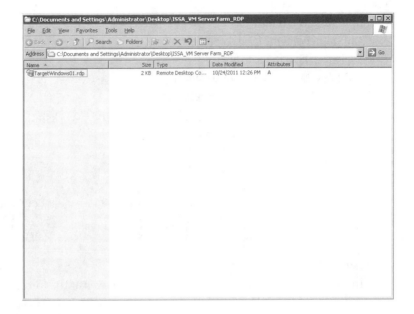

21. Log on to the **TargetWindows01 VM** server with the following credentials:
- User name: **Administrator**
- Password: **ISS316Security**

22. Click OK in the Connect to Server dialog box to start the FileZilla Server application.

This dialog box loads automatically when the Windows server starts, with the address and password already filled in.

FIGURE 7.9

Connect to Server
dialog box

23. **Minimize** the **FileZilla Server application**.

24. **Repeat steps 2-18** to create both secret and public keys on the TargetWindows01 desktop using the following information:
    - Name: **TargetWinVM01**
    - EMail: **targetwinvm01@vlabsolutions.com**
    - Passphrase: **ISS316Security**
    - Backup/export file name: **targetvm01**
    - Export certificate file name: **targetvm01_public**

25. **Minimize** the **TargetWindows01 window** to return to the vWorkstation desktop.

26. **Close** the **ISSA_VM Server Farm_RDP folder**.

> **Note:**
> The next steps will use the FileZilla application to transfer the TargetWindows01 public key to the vWorkstation desktop.

27. **Double-click** the **FileZilla icon**.

28. **Type** the following login credentials in the address boxes at the top of the application window that opens to connect to the FileZilla Server on the TargetWindows01 server.
    - Host: **172.30.0.8**
    - User name: **student**
    - Password: **ISS316Security**
    - Port: **21**

29. **Click** the **Quickconnect button** to connect to the FileZilla Server.

FIGURE 7.10

Connecting to
TargetWindows01 using
the FileZilla Client

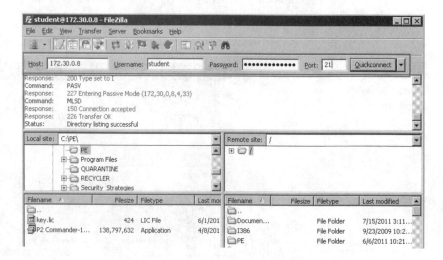

30. **Navigate** to the TargetWindows01 desktop (**C:/Documents and Settings/Administrator/Desktop**) in the right pane.

31. **Right-click** the **targetwinvm01_public.asc file** and **select Download** from the context menu.

32. **Minimize** the **FileZilla application**.

> **Note:**
> The next steps will import and configure the targetwinvm01_public key on the vWorkstation.

33. In the Kleopatra application, **click the Import Certificates button** in the toolbar.
34. In the Select Certificate File dialog box, **navigate** to the desktop and **select** the **targetwinvm01_public.asc file** and **click Open** to import the file.

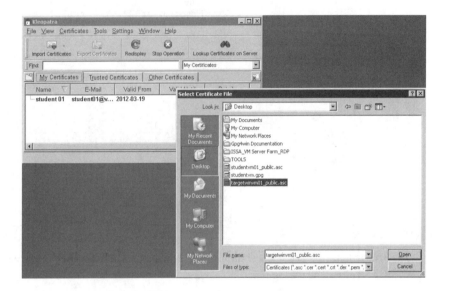

The targetwinvm01_public.asc file is now listed as a new line item on the Imported Certificates tab of the Kleopatra application.

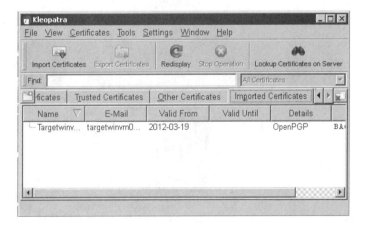

7

Relate Windows Encryption
and Hashing to Confidentiality
and Integrity

35. **Double-click** the **targetwinvm01_public line item** in Kleopatra to open the Certificate Details dialog box.
36. Click the **Trust Certificates made by this Certificate button** in the Actions section of the dialog box.

FIGURE 7.13

Trust Certificates option

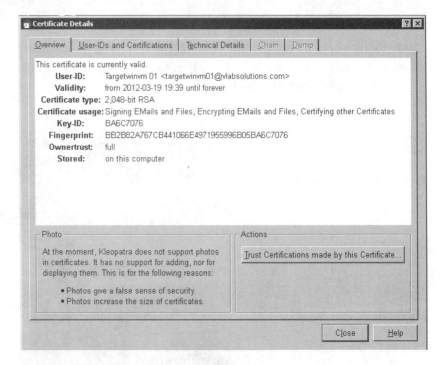

37. In the Change Trust Level dialog box, **select** the **I believe checks are very accurate radio button** and **click OK** to close the dialog box.

FIGURE 7.14

Completing the
certificate confirmation

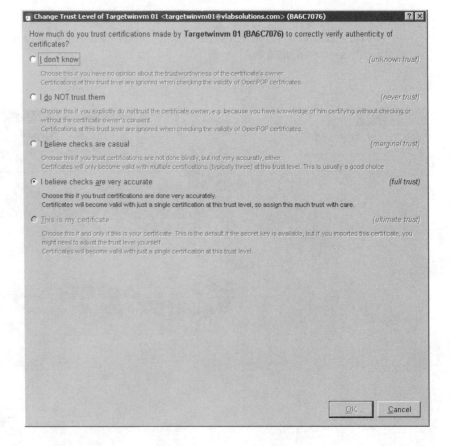

38. **Click OK** when prompted to confirm the changes.

39. **Click** the **Close button** to close the Certificate Details dialog box.

> **Note:**
> The next steps will create a file on the vWorkstation and encrypt it. Then you will transfer the file to the TargetWindows01 desktop.

40. **Open** a new document in the Notepad (**Start > Programs > Accessories > Notepad**).

41. **Type I like information systems security.** into the body of the document.

42. **Click File > Save** in the Notepad toolbar.

43. In the Save as dialog box, **name** the file **Lab 7** and **select Text Document [*.txt]** from the "Save as type" menu. **Click OK** to save the file to the vWorkstation desktop.

44. **Close** the **Notepad**.

45. **Right-click** the **Lab 7.txt file** on the vWorkstation desktop and select **Sign and encrypt** from the context menu.

FIGURE 7.15

Sign and encrypt option

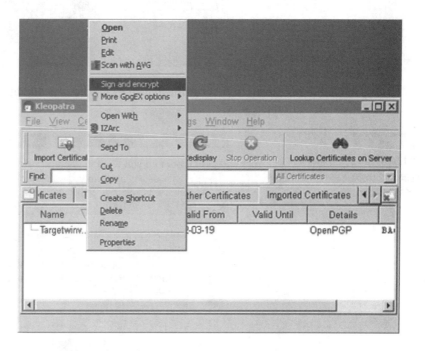

7

Relate Windows Encryption
and Hashing to Confidentiality
and Integrity

46. Click the **Remove unencrypted original file when done checkbox** at the bottom of the Sign/Encrypt Files dialog box and **click Next** to continue.

Encrypt a file

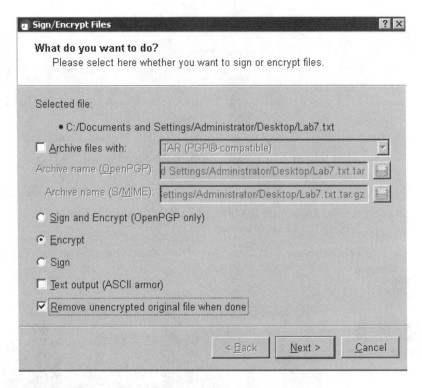

47. On the next screen, **click** the **first certificate name** and **click** the **Add button** to add it to the list of certificates to encrypt.

Add certificates as recipients to an encrypted file

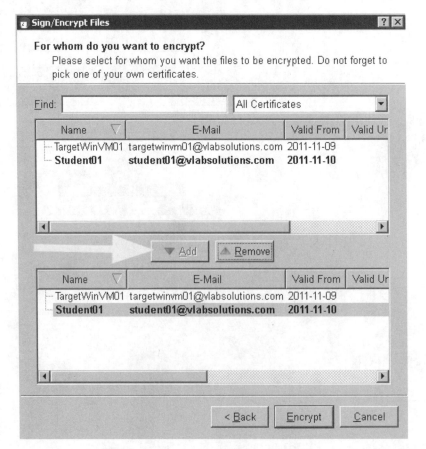

48. Click the **second certificate name** and **click** the **Add button**.

49. **Click** the **Encrypt button** to close the dialog box.

50. **Click Finish**.

    Once encrypted, the newly encrypted file replaces the original text file on the desktop.

51. Use the **File Transfer button** to **download** the **Lab 7.txt.gpg encrypted file** to your local computer and **submit** it as part of your deliverables.

52. **Maximize** the **FileZilla application**.

    You may find that the connection has timed out. Follow the connection and navigation instructions in step 28-30 above to reconnect before proceeding.

53. **Right-click** the **Lab 7.txt.gpg file** in the left pane and **select Upload** from the context menu to transfer it to the TargetWindows01 desktop.

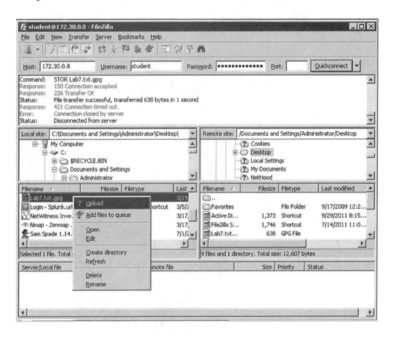

54. **Close** the **FileZilla application**.

> **Note:**
> The next steps will decrypt the file you just transferred. You will verify that the integrity of encrypted files is maintained during transmission by comparing the hash values before and after the transfer. You will then make a screen capture of the successful file decryption for use as a deliverable in this lab.

55. **Maximize** the **TargetWindows01 window** from the application tray.

56. **Right-click** the **Lab 7.txt.gpg file** on the TargetWindows01 desktop and **select Decrypt and verify** from the context menu.

FIGURE 7.20

Decrypt the Lab 7.txt. gpg file

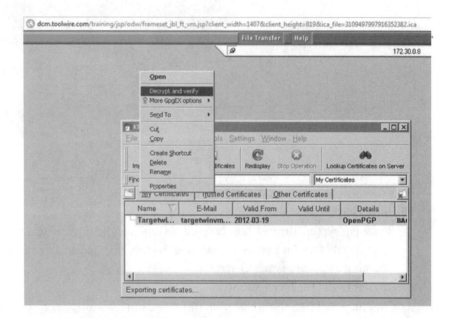

57. **Click** the **Decrypt/Verify button** at the bottom of the Decrypt/Verify Files dialog box.

58. When prompted, **type ISS316Security** (the passphrase you used when you created the encryption file) and **click OK**.

FIGURE 7.21

Entering a password to decrypt a file

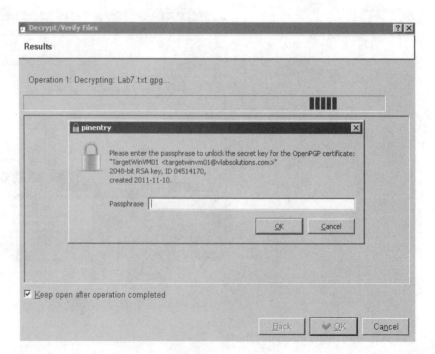

59. **Verify** that the file is successfully decrypted.

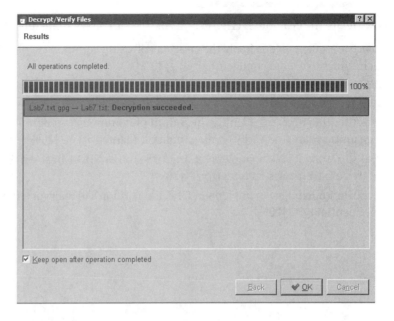

60. **Make a screen capture** of the successfully decrypted file and **paste** it into a new text document. **Submit** this file to your instructor as a deliverable.

> **Note:**
>
> To capture the screen, **press** the **Ctrl** and **PrtSc** keys together, and then **use Ctrl + V** to paste the image into a Word or other word processor document.

61. **Click OK** to close the Decrypt/Verify Files dialog box.
62. **Double-click** the **Lab 7.txt file** on the TargetWindows01 desktop and **verify** that the text in the file is the same as you typed in step 41 above.
63. **Close** the **Notepad**.
64. Use the **File Transfer button** to **download** the **decrypted Lab 7.txt file** to your local computer and **submit** it as part of your deliverables.
65. **Close** the **TargetWindows01 window** to return to the vWorkstation desktop.
66. **Close Kleopatra**.

Evaluation Criteria and Rubrics

The following are the evaluation criteria and rubrics for Lab #7 that students must perform:

1. Was the student able to apply the concepts of using common cryptographic and encryption techniques to ensure confidentiality? – [**20%**]

2. Was the student able to apply the concepts of hashing to ensure integrity of data transmission and data reception? – [**20%**]

3. Was the student able to identify the output of common cryptographic and hashing tools on transmitted data and verify confidentiality and integrity? – [**20%**]

4. Was the student able to implement an MD5 sum or SHA1 hash on a data transmission or message to verify data transmission integrity? – [**20%**]

5. Was the student able to implement GPG for Windows to encrypt a data message to ensure confidentiality? – [**20%**]

LAB #7 – ASSESSMENT WORKSHEET

Relate Windows Encryption and Hashing to Confidentiality and Integrity

Course Name and Number:
_____

Student Name:
_____

Instructor Name:
_____

Lab Due Date:
_____

Overview

This lab demonstrated how hashing tools can be used to ensure message and file transfer integrity and how encryption can be used to maximize confidentiality. Common hashing and encryption tools, including MD5, SHA1, and GnuPG, were used. You used GnuPG to generate both a public and private key and a secret key for encryption only.

Lab Assessment Questions & Answers

1. If you and another person want to encrypt messages, should you provide that person with your public key, private key, or both?

_____

_____

_____

_____

2. What does GPG allow you to do once it is installed?

_____

_____

_____

_____

3. Name two different types of encryption supported by GPG for your key.

_____

_____

_____

_____

4. What happens when you sign and trust a new key to your keychain?

_____

_____

_____

_____

5. If a user sends you his/her public key, will he/she be able to decrypt your encrypted messages once you import and sign his/her key?

_____

_____

_____

_____

6. What are the similarities between an MD5 hash and a fingerprint?

_____

_____

_____

_____

7. How would you encrypt a Web server and the pages it serves up?

_____

_____

_____

_____

8. Why is hashing all database inputs not considered encryption of the database? What value does hashing database entries provide?

_____

_____

_____

_____

9. Where would you remove a user's certificate from being able to access systems on your network?

_____

_____

_____

_____

10. Which connection type is secure and which is cleartext between SSH, Telnet, and FTP?

_____

_____

_____

_____

Perform a Website and Database Attack by Exploiting Identified Vulnerabilities

Introduction

In this lab, you will verify and perform a cross-site scripting (XSS) exploit and an SQL injection attack on the test bed Web application and Web server using the Damn Vulnerable Web Application (DVWA) found on the TargetUbuntu01 Linux VM server. You will use a Web browser and some simple command strings to identify the IP target host and its known vulnerabilities and exploits, and then attack the Web application and Web server using cross-site scripting (XSS) and an SQL injection to exploit the sample Web application running on that server.

Learning Objectives

Upon completing this lab, you will be able to:

- Identify Web application and Web server backend database vulnerabilities as viable attack vectors
- Develop an attack plan to compromise and exploit a website using cross-site scripting (XSS) against sample vulnerable Web applications
- Conduct a manual cross-site scripting (XSS) attack against sample vulnerable Web applications
- Perform SQL injection attacks against sample vulnerable Web applications with e-commerce data entry fields
- Mitigate known Web application and Web server vulnerabilities with security countermeasures to eliminate risk from compromise and exploitation

TOOLS AND SOFTWARE	
NAME	**MORE INFORMATION**
Damn Vulnerable Web Application (DVWA)	http://www.dvwa.co.uk

Deliverables

Upon completion of this lab, you are required to provide the following deliverables to your instructor:

1. A written report of the identified vulnerabilities, exploits, and remediation steps covered in this lab;
2. Screen capture of the cross-site scripting (XSS) attack;
3. Screen capture of the SQL injection attack;
4. Lab Assessment Questions & Answers for Lab #8.

Hands-On Steps

1. This lab begins at the student landing vWorkstation virtual machine desktop of the VSCL, as shown here.

FIGURE 8.1

"Student Landing" VSCL workstation

> **Note:**
> The next steps access the Damn Vulnerable Web Application (DVWA) using an Internet browser. You will change the security level of DVWA to low so that you will be able to perform the steps in the rest of the lab.

2. **Double-click** the **Mozilla Firefox icon** on the desktop to open the Firefox browser.

   You can access the DVWA tool using any Internet browser, but the steps in this lab will use the Firefox browser.

3. **Type http://172.30.0.4/dvwa** in the browser's address box and **press Enter**.

FIGURE 8.2

DVWA login screen

4. Log in to the application with the following credentials and **click Login** to continue:
   - Username: **admin**
   - Password: **password**
5. On the DVWA Welcome screen, **click** the **DVWA Security button**.
6. **Select low** from the Script Security drop-down menu. **Click Submit** to change the security level.

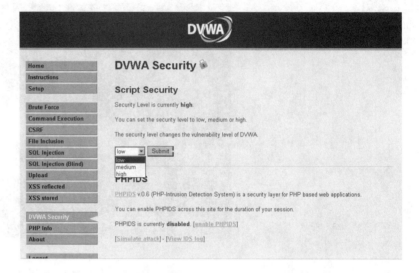

FIGURE 8.3

Changing the script
security level in DVWA

> **Note:**
> The next steps use the DVWA tool to perform an attack exploiting a cross-site scripting (XSS) vulnerability. The goal of an XSS attack is usually to gain administrator, or some other elevated level of, user privileges.

7. **Click** the **XSS reflected button** in the DVWA navigation menu.

   XSS vulnerabilities are generally found in Web forms that send and retrieve data to databases via HTML.

8. In the What's your name? box, **type Simon** and **click Submit**.

   The Web form will take the name you entered and repeat it back to you in a friendly welcome.

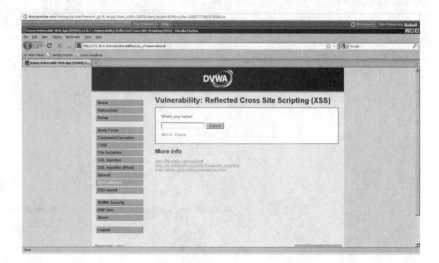

FIGURE 8.4

Expected output from
XSS test

9. In the What's your name? box, **type <this is a test>** and **click Submit**.

The Web form cannot handle the unexpected data and fails to return the expected outcome. You have uncovered a vulnerability in this form.

FIGURE 8.5

Testing the XSS reflected vulnerability

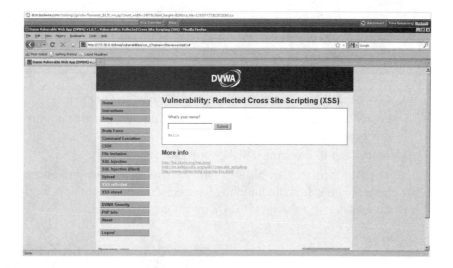

10. In the What's your name? box, **type <script>alert('vuln');</script> Hello!** and **click Submit**.

The Web form processed the script and returned a popup alert window.

FIGURE 8.6

Alert window processed by the Web form

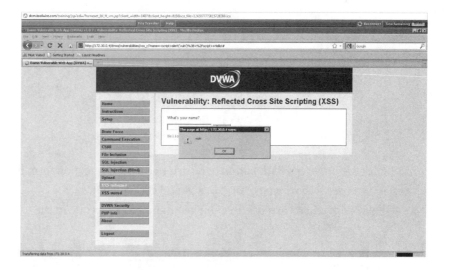

11. **Make a screen capture** showing the popup alert window and **paste** it into a new text document.

> **Note:**
>
> To capture the screen, **press** the **Ctrl** and **PrtSc** keys together, and then **use Ctrl + V** to paste the image into a Word or other word processor document.

12. Use the **File Transfer button** to **download** the **text document** to your local computer and **submit** it as part of your deliverables.

> **Note:**
> The next steps will insert a series of SQL statements into a Web form to find and then exploit an SQL injection vulnerability. Many of these commands will not return any errors. Experienced hackers will continue probing until they find the data they were seeking.

13. **Click** the **SQL Injection button** in the DVWA navigation menu.

    Poorly designed and secured Web forms can be exploited to output passwords, credit card information, and other data.

14. In the User ID box, **type O'Malley** and **click Submit**.

    The Web form was unable to handle the special character of an apostrophe. Often, programmers forget to include script handling for special characters in data input forms. This type of error can make an application vulnerable to SQL injection.

FIGURE 8.7

SQL error

15. **Click** the **browser's Back button** to return to the SQL Injection form in DVWA.

16. In the User ID box, **type a' OR 'x'='x';#** and **click Submit**.

    This script will return the first and last names of everyone in the application's database.

FIGURE 8.8

Results from the SQL injection test

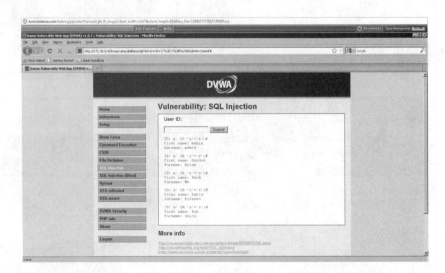

17. In the User ID box, **type a' ORDER BY 1;#** and **click Submit**.

    Review the output. If there is no error indicating an SQL injection vulnerability, proceed to the next step. If you see an error statement, **click** the **browser's Back button** and proceed to step 20.

18. In the User ID box, **type a' ORDER BY 2;#** and **click Submit**.

    Review the output. If there is no error indicating an SQL injection vulnerability, proceed to the next step. If you see an error statement, **click** the **browser's Back button** and proceed to step 20.

19. In the User ID box, **type a' ORDER BY 3;#** and **click Submit**.

    Review the output. If there is no error indicating an SQL injection vulnerability, proceed to the next step. If you see an error statement, **click** the **browser's Back button** and proceed to step 20.

20. In the User ID box, **type a' OR firstname IS NULL;#** and **click Submit**.

    The error message indicates that the field name is spelled wrong.

FIGURE 8.9

Results from the "firstname" test

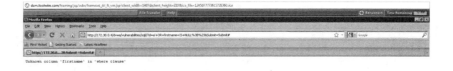

21. **Click** the **browser's Back button**.

22. In the User ID box, **type a' OR first_name IS NULL;#** and **click Submit** to try another common spelling for the name of this field.

    The lack of an error message indicates that the field name is now spelled correctly.

23. In the User ID box, **type a' OR database() LIKE 'DB';#** and **click Submit**.

    This script searches for a possible hit on the database's characters.

24. In the User ID box, **type a' OR database() LIKE 'd%';#** and **click Submit**.

    Like the previous script, this one searches for a possible hit on the database's characters, but the percent sign (%) will split the fields.

25. **Click** the **browser's Back button**.

26. In the User ID box, **type a' UNION SELECT table_schema, table_name FROM information_Schema.tables;#** and **click Submit**.

    This script will return all of the table and column names in the database.

FIGURE 8.10

Results from the "table_schema, table_name" test

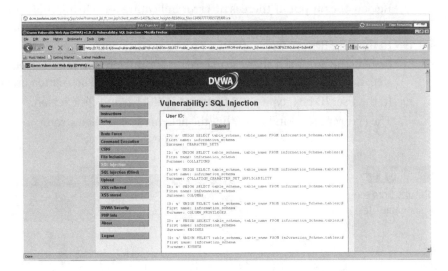

27. In the User ID box, **type a' UNION ALL SELECT 1, @@version;#** and **click Submit**.

    This script will return information about the version of SQL being used on the server.

FIGURE 8.11

Results from the "@@version" test

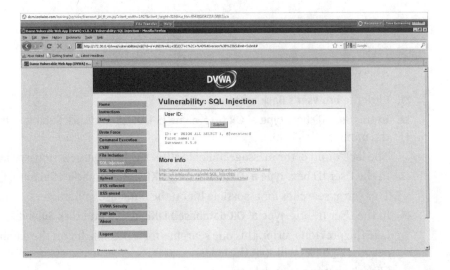

28. In the User ID box, **type a' UNION ALL SELECT system_user(), user();#** and **click Submit**.

    This script will return information about the user name that you are using as you make queries on the server.

29. In the User ID box, **type a' UNION ALL SELECT user, password FROM mysql.user;# priv;# '** and **click Submit**.

    This script will give you a hash for the user to the backend database.

30. **Make a screen capture** showing the hash information and **paste** it into a new text document.

 Note:

To capture the screen, **press** the **Ctrl** and **PrtSc** keys together, and then **use Ctrl + V** to paste the image into a Word or other word processor document.

---

31. Use the **File Transfer button** to **download** the **text document** to your local computer and **submit** it as part of your deliverables.

32. In the User ID box, **type 'UNION SELECT 'test', '123' INTO OUTFILE 'testing1.txt** and **click Submit**.

    This script will indicate that the data can be written to a file. Together with the information you gathered in earlier tests, you now have a user with elevated permissions, user IDs, passwords, and table and column information—in other words, an injectable database.

33. **Close** the **Firefox browser** to exit DVWA.

 Note:

These test scripts were all typed in cleartext. Often hackers will use hexadecimal character strings instead of cleartext to make the scripts harder to detect.

Evaluation Criteria and Rubrics

The following are the evaluation criteria and rubrics for Lab #8 that students must perform:

1. Was the student able to identify Web application and Web server backend database vulnerabilities as viable attack vectors? – [**20%**]

2. Was the student able to develop an attack plan to compromise and exploit a website using cross-site scripting (XSS) against sample vulnerable Web applications? – [**20%**]

3. Was the student able to conduct a manual cross-site scripting (XSS) attack against sample vulnerable Web applications? – [**20%**]

4. Was the student able to perform SQL injection attacks against sample vulnerable Web applications with e-commerce data entry fields? – [**20%**]

5. Was the student able to mitigate known Web application and Web server vulnerabilities with security countermeasures to eliminate risk from compromise and exploitation? – [**20%**]

LAB #8 – ASSESSMENT WORKSHEET

Perform a Website and Database Attack by Exploiting Identified Vulnerabilities

Course Name and Number:
_____

Student Name:
_____

Instructor Name:
_____

Lab Due Date:
_____

Overview

In this lab, you verified and performed a cross-site scripting (XSS) exploit and an SQL injection attack on the test bed Web application and Web server using the Damn Vulnerable Web Application (DVWA) found on the TargetUbuntu01 Linux VM server. You first identified the IP target host, identified known vulnerabilities and exploits, and then attacked the Web application and Web server using XSS and an SQL injection to exploit the Web application using a Web browser and some simple command strings.

Lab Assessment Questions & Answers

1. Why is it critical to perform a penetration test on a Web application and a Web server prior to production implementation?

   _____

   _____

   _____

   _____

2. What is a cross-site scripting attack? Explain in your own words.

   _____

   _____

   _____

   _____

3. What is a reflective cross-site scripting attack?

_____

_____

_____

_____

4. What common method of obfuscation is used in most real-world SQL attacks?

_____

_____

_____

_____

5. Which Web application attack is more prone to extracting privacy data elements out of a database?

_____

_____

_____

_____

6. If you can monitor when SQL injections are performed on an SQL database, what would you recommend as a security countermeasure to monitor your production SQL databases?

_____

_____

_____

_____

7. Given that Apache and Internet Information Services (IIS) are the two most popular Web application servers for Linux and Microsoft® Windows platforms, what would you do to identify known software vulnerabilities and exploits?

_____

_____

_____

_____

8. What can you do to ensure that your organization incorporates penetration testing and Web application testing as part of its implementation procedures?

_____

_____

_____

_____

9. What other security countermeasures do you recommend for websites and Web application deployment to ensure the CIA of the Web application?

_____

_____

_____

_____

_____

_____

_____

_____

10. Who is responsible and accountable for the CIA of production Web applications and Web servers?

_____

_____

_____

_____

Perform a Virus Scan and Malware Identification Scan and Eliminate Threats

Introduction

In this lab, you will learn how to use the AVG anti-virus software to identify malware found on a compromised system. You will also examine the services enabled in the Windows vWorkstation machine and disable any unnecessary applications and services. Finally, you will examine and document the default configurations of a Windows workstation internal firewall.

Learning Objectives

Upon completing this lab, you will be able to:

- Identify the risks associated with viruses, malware, and malicious software on a Windows server
- Apply security countermeasures to mitigate the risk caused by viruses, malware, and malicious software
- Enable AVG as an anti-virus, malware, and malicious software security countermeasure on a Windows server
- Disable unnecessary services in a Windows workstation and enable needed services
- Configure a Windows workstation internal firewall to enable/disable ports, applications, and services

TOOLS AND SOFTWARE	
NAME	**MORE INFORMATION**
AVG	http://free.avg.com/us-en/homepage
IZarc Archiver	http://www.izarc.org/

Deliverables

Upon completion of this lab, you are required to provide the following deliverables to your instructor:

1. Text document that contains the following information:
   a. a screen capture of the AVG Virus Vault displaying the file you added in this lab;
   b. a screen capture showing all of the services that were disabled in this lab;
   c. a screen capture of the Windows Internal Firewall showing the changes you made in this lab;
2. Lab Assessment Questions & Answers for Lab #9.

Hands-On Steps

1. This lab begins at the student landing vWorkstation virtual machine desktop of the VSCL, as shown here.

"Student Landing" VSCL workstation

> **Note:**
> The next steps use AVG to run a virus scan on the Windows vWorkstation machine to identify malware. You will open an encrypted file using the IZarc Archiver tool and then quarantine and delete an infected file.

2. **Double-click** the **My Computer icon** on the desktop.
3. **Double-click** the **Local Disk (C:) icon** in the My Computer window.
4. **Double-click** the **Security_Strategies folder**.
5. **Double-click** the **ISSA_TOOLS folder**.
6. **Verify** that the **prodrev.zip file** appears in the folder. This encrypted zip file will be used later in the lab.

FIGURE 9.2

Locating the prodrev. zip file

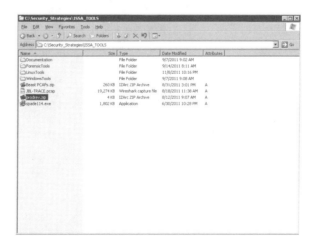

7. **Minimize** the **ISSA_TOOLS folder**.
8. **Double-click** the **AVG 2012** icon on the desktop to start the anti-virus application.
9. **Click** the **Update Now button** from the application's navigation bar.

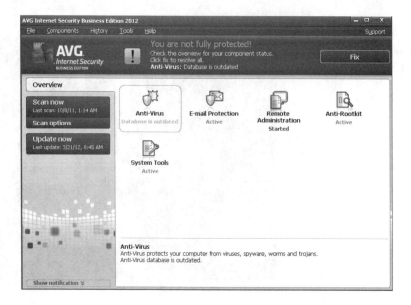

This computer does not have direct access to the Internet, so selecting this option will have no effect in the lab and you will see a warning message in the applications header area throughout this part of the lab. However, this is an important step in performing a virus scan outside the lab, so it is included here.

10. **Click** the **Scan options button** in the navigation bar and **click Change scan settings** under the Scan specific files or folders section of the page.

11. **Accept** the **default settings** on the first screen of the wizard and **click Next** to continue.

FIGURE 9.5

Default scan settings

12. **Navigate** to the ISSA_TOOLS folder (**C:/Security_Strategies/ISSA_TOOLS**) and **click** the **checkbox** in front of the folder.

Because ISSA_TOOLS is a subfolder of the Security_Strategies folder, AVG will automatically select the Security_Strategies folder for scanning as well as all of the subfolders under the ISSA_TOOLS folder.

FIGURE 9.6

Selected folders
for scanning

13. **Click** the **Start specific scan button** to begin the scanning process and remove any identified threats.

    When the scan is completed, AVG will display a screen indicating any threats that it identified. Notice that the tool did not identify the prodrev.zip file because anti-virus software cannot open encrypted files for scanning.

FIGURE 9.7

Scan summary for completed scan

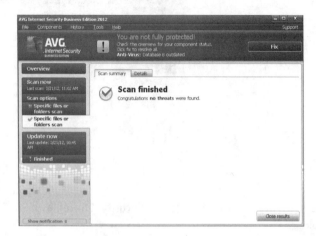

14. **Maximize** the **ISSA_TOOLS folder**.
15. **Right-click** the **prodrev.zip file**.
16. **Click IZarc** and **Extract Here** from the context menu.

FIGURE 9.8

Extracting the encrypted file

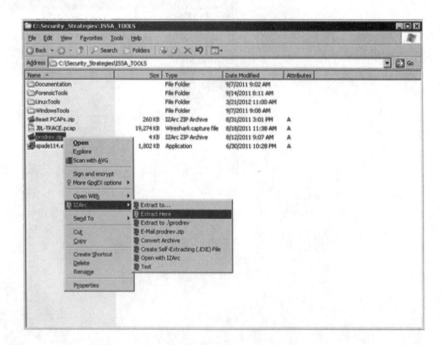

17. When prompted, **type password123** (the document's password) in the password dialog box.

    The newly extracted file, productreview.pdf, will appear in the ISSA_TOOLS folder.

18. **Double-click** the **productreview.pdf file** and **type password123** (the document's password) in the password dialog box to open the file.

    AVG, still running in the background, will detect the virus within the file and display an alert message.

AVG's Threat
Detected alert

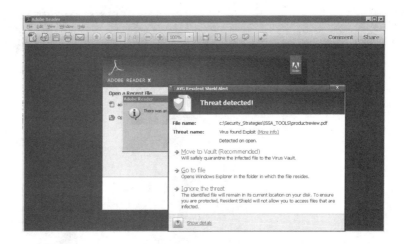

19. **Click** the **Move to Vault (Recommended)** option to quarantine the file within AVG's vault.

20. **Click Close** to close the alert message.

21. **Click OK** to close the Adobe error message and **close Adobe Reader**.

22. **Close** the **ISSA_TOOLS folder** to bring the AVG software to the forefront.

23. In the AVG toolbar, **click History** and **select Virus Vault**.

24. **Expand** the **Path to file column width** as necessary to **verify** that the **productreview.pdf file** is displayed in the vault.

The AVG Virus Vault

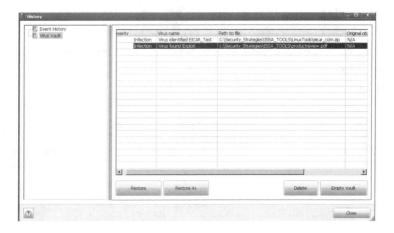

25. **Click** the **Empty Vault button** to delete any virus, malware, and malicious software detected by the application.

26. **Click Yes** to confirm the process.

27. **Click Close** to close the Virus Vault.

28. **Click** the **Scan options button** in the navigation bar and **click** the **Whole computer scan option**.

   This second scan will confirm that any threats have been removed from the computer. **Verify** that all threats were removed.

FIGURE 9.11

Whole computer scan results

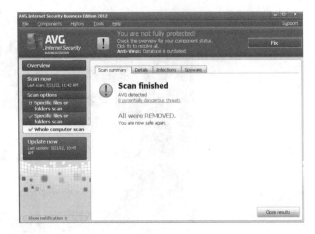

29. **Click Close results** to return to the AVG main screen.
30. **Close** the **AVG window**.

> **Note:**
> The next steps will disable and document the unwanted services that are running on the vWorkstation virtual machine.

31. **Right-click** the **My Computer icon** on the desktop and **select Manage** from the context menu.
32. **Double-click** the **Services and Applications icon** in the right pane of the Computer Management window.
33. **Double-click** the **Services icon** in the right pane.

   A list of the services running on this virtual machine is displayed in the right pane. The Startup Type column indicates whether those services start automatically or manually, or whether they have been disabled.

FIGURE 9.12

Default view of the services running on this computer

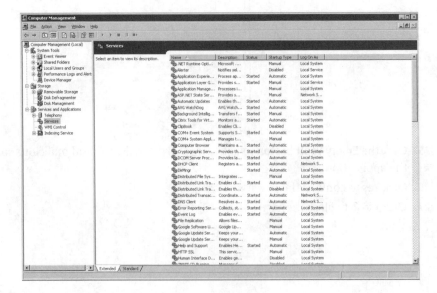

34. **Make a screen capture** of the complete list of services on the Extended tab (the default view) and **paste** it into a new text document. Notice that you may have to use the scrollbar on the right of the window to see the complete list.

> **Note:**
> To capture the screen, **press** the **Ctrl** and **PrtSc** keys together, and then **use Ctrl + V** to paste the image into a Word or other word processor document.

35. **Click** the **Standard tab** to display the standard services.
36. **Make a screen capture** of the complete list of services on the Services tab and **paste** it into the text document. Notice that you may have to use the scrollbar on the right of the window to see the complete list.
37. Use the **File Transfer button** to **download** the **text file** to your local computer and **submit** it as part of your deliverables.
38. **Click** the **Extended tab** to return to the original view.
39. **Double-click** the **Wireless Configuration Properties** service (use the scrollbar to locate the service in the list, if necessary).
40. In the Wireless Configuration Properties dialog box, **select Disabled** from the drop-down menu in the Startup type section.
41. **Click OK** to change the Startup type.

FIGURE 9.13

Changing the
Startup type

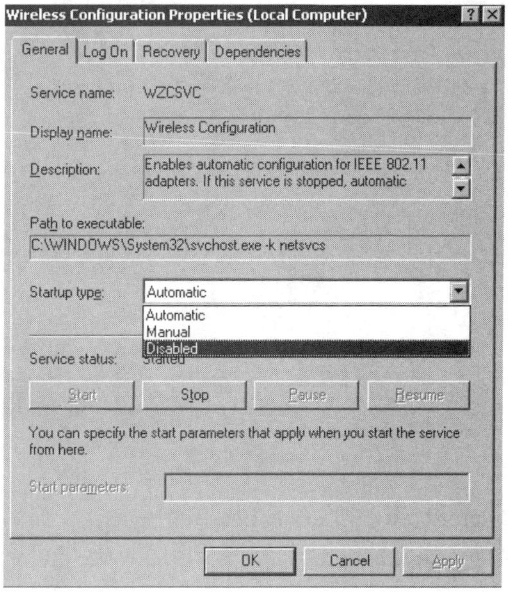

42. **Close** the **Computer Management window.**

> **Note:**
> The next steps will configure the Windows Internal Firewall to enable or disable ports and applications on a Windows server. A firewall, when enabled, can block outside sources from being able to insert malware and viruses.

43. **Click** the **Windows Start button,** then **click Settings** and **select Control Panel** from the menu.

44. In the Control Panel, **double-click** the **Windows Firewall**.

    The Windows Firewall on this computer is set to Off.

45. **Click** the **On radio button** to enable the Windows Firewall.

    By default, the Windows Firewall disables several important services like file transfer protocol (FTP), remote desktop protocol (RDP), and Internet Control Message Protocol (ICMP) which includes the Ping command. You will need to manually enable those services.

FIGURE 9.14

Enabling the Windows Firewall

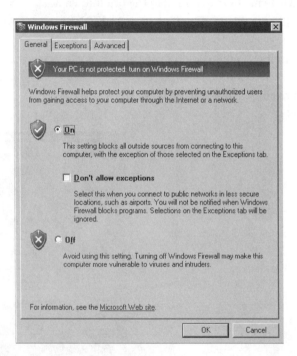

46. **Click** the **Advanced tab** to change these settings.

47. **Click** the **Settings button** in the ICMP section of the dialog box.

48. **Click** the **Allow incoming echo request checkbox.**

49. **Make a screen capture** of the changes you made on the ICMP Settings dialog box and **paste** it into a new text document.

50. **Click OK** to allow ping replies and close the dialog box.

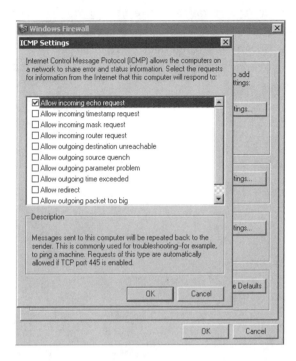

51. **Click** the **Settings button** in the Network Connection Settings section of the dialog box.
52. **Click** the **FTP Server checkbox** and **click OK** on the Service Settings dialog box to enable the FTP service.
53. **Click** the **Remote Desktop checkbox** and **click OK** on the Service Settings dialog box to enable the remote desktop service.

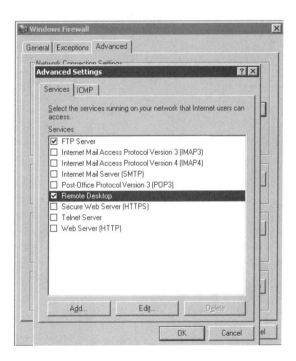

54. **Make a screen capture** of the changes you made in the Advanced Settings dialog box and **paste** it into the text document.

55. Use the **File Transfer button** to **download** the **text file** to your local computer and **submit** it as part of your deliverables.

56. **Click OK** to close the Advanced Settings dialog box.

57. **Click OK** to close the Windows Firewall.

58. **Close** the **Control Panel**.

Evaluation Criteria and Rubrics

The following are the evaluation criteria and rubrics for Lab #9 that students must perform:

1. Was the student able to identify the risks associated with viruses, malware, and malicious software on a Windows server? – [**20%**]

2. Was the student able to apply security countermeasures to mitigate the risk caused by viruses, malware, and malicious software? – [**20%**]

3. Was the student able to enable AVG as an anti-virus, malware, and malicious software security countermeasure on a Windows server? – [**20%**]

4. Was the student able to disable unnecessary services in a Windows workstation and enable needed services? – [**20%**]

5. Was the student able to configure a Windows workstation internal firewall to enable/disable ports, applications, and services? – [**20%**]

LAB #9 – ASSESSMENT WORKSHEET

Perform a Virus Scan and Malware Identification Scan and Eliminate Threats

Course Name and Number:

_____

Student Name:

_____

Instructor Name:

_____

Lab Due Date:

_____

Overview

In this lab, you learned how to use the AVG anti-virus software to identify malware found on a compromised system. You also examined the services enabled in the Windows vWorkstation machine and disabled any unnecessary applications and services. Finally, you examined and documented the default configurations of a Windows workstation internal firewall.

Lab Assessment Questions & Answers

1. What is the main difference between a virus and a Trojan?

_____

_____

_____

_____

2. A virus or malware can impact which of the three tenets of information systems security (CIA)? Describe how it impacts it as well.

_____

_____

_____

_____

3. Once a malicious file is found on your computer, what are the default settings for USB/removable device scanning? What should an organization do regarding use of USB hard drives and slots on existing computers and devices?

_____

_____

_____

_____

4. Why is it recommended to do an anti-virus signature file update before performing an anti-virus scan on your computer?

_____

_____

_____

_____

5. When sending a file, a user asks you to zip it and encrypt the file, if possible. Why would this be?

_____

_____

_____

_____

6. You receive an e-mail regarding a link from one of your friends for some special documents. Shortly after that you receive the same e-mail from three other friends and the e-mails are not being blocked. What is the likely cause?

_____

_____

_____

_____

7. Specify a setting you would want to turn on if you were running AVG on your system to improve the quality of scans you do on the system.

_____

_____

_____

_____

8. Your employees e-mail file attachments to each other and externally through the organization's firewall and Internet connection. What security countermeasures can you implement to help mitigate the risk of rogue e-mail attachments and URL Web links?

_____

_____

_____

_____

_____

9. What are typical indicators that your computer system is compromised?

_____

_____

_____

_____

_____

10. What elements are needed in a workstation domain policy regarding use of anti-virus and malicious software prevention tools?

_____

_____

_____

_____

_____

_____

Craft an Information Systems Security Policy

Introduction

Information systems security policy defines an organization's attitude toward information, and announces internally and externally that information is an asset, the organization's property, and it is to be protected from unauthorized access, modification, disclosure, and destruction. In this lab, you will review a security policy development guide provided by the SANS Institute, and then research existing information security policies and templates. You also will draft a business continuity plan policy for Online Goodies, a fictitious e-commerce company, that will ensure risk is minimized and that any security incidents are handled effectively.

This lab is a paper-based design lab and does not require use of the Virtual Security Cloud Lab (VSCL). To successfully complete the deliverables for this lab, you will need access to a text editor or word processor, such as Microsoft® Word. For some labs, you may also need access to a graphics line drawing application, such as Visio or PowerPoint.

> **Note:**
> If you don't have a word processor or graphics package, use OpenOffice on the student landing vWorkstation for your lab deliverables and to answer the lab assessment questions. To capture screenshots, **press Prt Sc > MSPAINT, paste** into a text document, and **save** the document in the Security_Strategies folder (**C:\Security_Strategies**) using the File Transfer function.

Learning Objectives and Outcomes

Upon completing this lab, you will be able to:

- Identify key elements of an information systems security policy definition
- Align a large organization's business continuity plan requirements into a policy definition criteria
- Craft an information systems security policy definition template for an organization's business continuity plan (BCP)
- Document an information systems security policy definition for an organization's business continuity plan (BCP)
- Assess how best to implement the business continuity plan (BCP) policy definition given the organization's culture and employees

Deliverables

Upon completion of this lab, you are required to provide the following deliverables to your instructor:

1. Business Continuity Plan Policy;
2. Lab Assessment Questions & Answers for Lab #10.

Hands-On Steps

1. This lab is a continuation of the business continuity planning process that you began in Lab #6. **Locate** a copy of the **Business Continuity Planning Lab #6** document that you submitted as a deliverable for that lab.

> **Note:**
> The next steps will guide you through the steps you will take to create a business continuity plan policy that meets your company's needs.

2. In a new text document, **create** a **business continuity plan policy.**

   You will follow the steps in this lab to complete the policy document as if you were part of the network administration team for Online Goodies. You will be responsible for determining what to document in this deliverable.

3. **Review** the **Preparation Guide to Information Security Policies White Paper.pdf** handout for this lab. The document from the SANS Institute suggests basic concepts, common security threats, and key components necessary to facilitate the process of developing security policies for your organization.

   If not available from your instructor, **use** the **File Transfer button** on the vWorkstation virtual machine to download this file from the Security_Strategies folder (**C:\Security_Strategies\Documentation\ Preparation Guide to Information Security Policies White Paper.pdf**).

4. From a workstation with Internet capability, **double-click** the **Internet browser icon** to open a browser session.

5. From the browser's search box, **type business continuity plan policy template** and **select** a **template** from the available options.

   Policy templates are also available from the SANS Institute (http://www.sans.org/security-resources/ policies).

6. In your text document, **draft** a **business continuity plan policy** for Online Goodies based on the template that you selected in step 5 above, and the scenario described in Lab #6.

7. In your text document, **draft** an **executive summary section** that explains the policy life cycle as described by the white paper you reviewed in step 3 above, and the importance of information security . policies for an e-commerce organization such as Online Goodies.

8. **Submit** the **text document** to your instructor as a deliverable for this lab.

10

Craft an Information
Systems Security Policy

Evaluation Criteria and Rubrics

The following are the evaluation criteria and rubrics for Lab #10 that the students must perform:

1. Was the student able to identify key elements of an information systems security policy definition? – [**20%**]

2. Was the student able to align a large organization's business continuity plan requirements into a policy definition criteria? – [**20%**]

3. Was the student able to craft an information systems security policy definition template for an organization's business continuity plan (BCP)? – [**20%**]

4. Was the student able to document an information systems security policy definition for an organization's business continuity plan (BCP)? – [**20%**]

5. Was the student able to assess how best to implement the business continuity plan (BCP) policy definition given the organization's culture and employees? – [**20%**]

LAB #10 – ASSESSMENT WORKSHEET

Craft an Information Systems Security Policy

Course Name and Number:
_____

Student Name:
_____

Instructor Name:
_____

Lab Due Date:
_____

Overview

Information systems security policy defines an organization's attitude toward information, and announces internally and externally that information is an asset, the organization's property, and it is to be protected from unauthorized access, modification, disclosure, and destruction. In this lab, you reviewed a security policy development guide provided by the SANS Institute, and then researched existing information security policies and templates. You also drafted a business continuity plan policy for Online Goodies, a fictitious e-commerce company, that ensures risk is minimized and that any security incidents are handled effectively.

Lab Assessment Questions & Answers

1. What is a policy? Give an example of an information systems security policy.

_____

_____

_____

_____

2. What is a standard? Give an example of an information systems security standard.

_____

_____

_____

_____

3. What is a guideline?

_____

_____

_____

_____

4. Name five different sample policy templates available through the SANS Institute.

_____

_____

_____

_____

_____

_____

_____

_____

5. What do you recommend as a strategy for implementation of this policy definition for the scenario provided in Lab #6 for an e-commerce organization?

_____

_____

_____

_____

6. Which policy template that you found on the SANS Institute site did you use for this BCP policy definition?

_____

_____

_____

_____

7. Why is it critical to define responsibilities and accountabilities in a BCP policy definition?

_____

_____

_____

_____

8. What are the five elements of an organization policy life cycle?

_____

_____

_____

_____

9. True or False: HIPAA Compliance and PCI DSS Compliance require documented and defined information systems security policies, including a BCP.

_____

_____

_____

_____

10. Why is policy enforcement required?

_____

_____

_____

_____